The Seventh Level

Designing Your Extraordinary Life

Joe Hefferon

BALBOA.
PRESS

A DIVISION OF HAY HOUSE

ISBN: 978-1-4525-5264-4 (sc)
ISBN: 978-1-4525-5270-5 (hc)
ISBN: 978-1-4525-5265-1 (e)
Library of Congress Control Number: 2012909078

Balboa Press books may be ordered through booksellers or by contacting:

Balboa Press
A Division of Hay House
1663 Liberty Drive
Bloomington, IN 47403
www.balboapress.com
1-(877) 407-4847

Because of the dynamic nature of the Internet, any web addresses or links contained in this book may have changed since publication and may no longer be valid. The views expressed in this work are solely those of the author and do not necessarily reflect the views of the publisher, and the publisher hereby disclaims any responsibility for them.

The author of this book does not dispense medical advice or prescribe the use of any technique as a form of treatment for physical, emotional, or medical problems without the advice of a physician, either directly or indirectly. The intent of the author is only to offer information of a general nature to help you in your quest for emotional and spiritual well-being. In the event you use any of the information in this book for yourself, which is your constitutional right, the author and the publisher assume no responsibility for your actions.

Printed in the United States of America

Balboa Press rev. date: 06/11/2012

Table of Contents

For Betty Ann

Acknowledgements

It's humbling to think about the many friends and supporters who helped me complete this book. I deeply appreciate what they have done for me. So in no particular order, here goes...

For the core idea I offer my gratitude to the architects and architecture critics who unwittingly assisted me through their wisdom and prevision. The well-layered breadth of their work and contribution to society is incalculable.

Thanks to my mother, Jean, for staying cancer free, leaving me with one less worry while I work and to my children, Kaitlin & Jackson, for giving me purpose. Kaitlin's honest advice made this a better book.

To my cousin Greg Carolan for his hysterical take on life; Steve & Sandee Torrioni, for their friendship and help in reading the manuscript; Roy McMakin for being patient in crafting my interview questions; Eric Worre & Randy Gage for their relentless business drive and Karen Tse, who gave me a new perspective on courage.

There were other writers who assisted me as well, especially Brad Parks who made me feel like part of the club; Jane Macdougall, Lahle Wolfe, Elizabeth Moore and Michael Ebeling.

And finally to Dr. Debbie Berebichez for her insight and for reminding me I was doing the right thing - to press on despite the obstacles; Ana Maria Manzo for trusting dreams and cheering my project; and Professor Dan Ariely, for allowing me to tell his story.

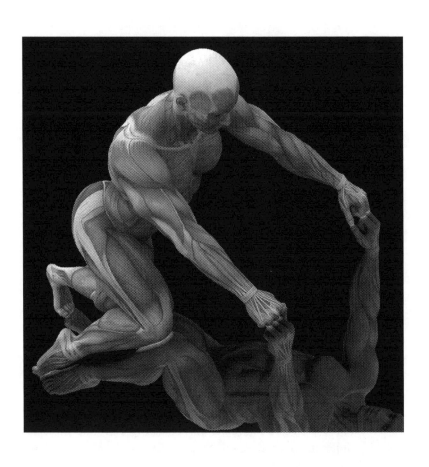

The Architecture of Human Endeavor

"Architecture is man's great sense of himself embodied in a world of his own making." – Frank Lloyd Wright

"The explosion comes from out of nowhere. Flames surround me. I can't see through the glowing white light of burning magnesium. Instinctively, I back away from the flames. Smoke permeates the room and although I can hardly see, I know my T-shirt is on fire. As if in a dream, I use my hands to put it out. Time slows down. I am thinking what to do next. Someone calls from the other side of the room and tries to guide me toward an exit. Realizing I am trapped, the flames bursting between the door and me, I run through the fire in order to escape. When I reach the exit, my clothes are once again in flames. I remove the burning remains of my shoes, T-shirt, and trousers and make my way outside. There, standing in charred socks and underwear, I drop down to the safety of the cold stone floor and look down at my hands. The right one is completely black, but still has its familiar shape, and thus I am relieved, assuming (incorrectly as I would later discover) that it is generally fine. Looking to the left, the picture is very different. Large pieces of skin hang loosely from my left arm. The whole arm itself is white as the stone floor beneath me, with particles of ash contrasting clearly against the perfect white skin. Only then does the unbearable pain in my arms and legs overcome me. Trying to minimize my pain, I lie as still as I can, even measuring my breath in order to eliminate any unnecessary movements. Soon the medical team arrives and carries me away."

That passage is from Professor Dan Ariely's horrific account of an explosion that left him with third degree burns over 70% of his body. In his paper, "Painful Lessons," (January 30, 2008) Ariely describes how he faced daily pain for three years in the hospital, enduring the torturous whole-body disinfectant dips, the ripping off and re-bandaging of his raw flesh and exposed nerves, along with countless surgeries. "During my hospitalization, pain, helplessness, fear and hopelessness were frequent and recurring emotions..."

Despite the physical pain of rehabilitation, coupled with mortifying social awkwardness, Dan Ariely flourished in academic pursuits. "During my first year in college, I was still wearing my Jobst suit, a head-to-toe elastic cover designed to create pressure on the recovering tissue, and which covered me completely with a brownish elastic panty hose-like material, leaving only holes for my eyes, ears and mouth. The image the Jobst suit created on me was somewhere between a Martian and a bank robber."

Dan began to feel that when people observed him, they somehow equated his damaged body with an equally diminished level of intelligence. Rather than have this inference be self-defeating, he saw it as an opportunity to prove his intellectual worth, and a way to re-establish his self-image.

What Dan Ariely focused on has subsequently brought him notoriety, a sense of humor, a best-selling book ("Predictably Irrational: The Hidden Forces that Shape Our Decisions" – Harper Collins, February 2008), and a remarkably unpretentious courage.

"Losing my appearance made me feel a strong separation between body and mind, and since one part of this duality did not reflect who I considered myself to be, I held on to the part that was not changed – the part that still held the true definition of myself – my mind, ideas, and way of thinking.

Overall, I try to look at my injury as another experience, one of the many that composes my life. This was indeed a powerful, painful, and prolonged experience, but it has also provided one of the most central "threads" of the way I understand myself and others. In retrospect, it is surprising to see how positively my life has turned out. I think it has turned out to be better than others expected and definitely better than I myself expected."

Today, a happily married Dan Ariely still struggles with pain and a tired, often uncooperative body, yet he finds happiness in his personal life and professional fulfillment from his research, teaching and writing. He challenges our assumptions about decision-making, dealing with pain, obstacles to success and rational thought. He does so with a subtle wit and underplayed intellectual arsenal.

What happened to Dan is unfathomable to nearly all of us. None of us can know how we would deal with such a tragedy unless we were to experience it, but we can learn deep, lasting lessons from Dan and others like him who grind it out, week by week, day by day, and manage not just to survive but to produce. He is a quiet hero.

Dan inspires me because he didn't set out to be heroic. The opportunity was heaped upon him and instead of letting it crush him, he clawed his way through it, to the life he deserves to live. I believe we all have the ability to get gritty, to find the passion to do something right now that makes today better than yesterday, and give us hope for a better tomorrow. The majority of us do not need to overcome a personal tragedy to move forward, but certainly there are some obstacles; real, perceived and misunderstood, that we need to get past. Most of us have a practiced list of excuses that have kept us stagnant. Yet for those of us in middle age, there is a nagging feeling that we still have time to get it right. We need to make those opportunities and stop waiting for them. With the right plan, proven methods and a little inspiration, you can get that rusty flywheel of yours spinning again. Before you know it, you'll actually be looking forward to the morning so you can get back to work.

Barbara Strauch, author of "The Secret Life of the Middle Aged Brain", says that because of minor hiccups in brain function, such as forgetting names or why we entered a room, we think our overall brainpower in diminishing. Her book demolishes those misconceptions. Our brains actually function better as we get older and our aptitude for learning new things is increased by our collective life experiences. Rather than looking for cemetery plots, we should be relishing our prime and enjoying the perks of our seasoned brains.

For those of you who have been under-productive, or just want to try something new, there is good news; I have a plan for you. You can do this. I promise. I will walk you through the process of building something you can be proud of. It will take effort for sure, but we will have fun early on and then progress into the rewards of work. And although it's the hard work that scares most of us back on to the couch, fear not, for this will have a happy ending. Now put the remote down and follow closely.

The Gulf

Have you ever noticed a constant low-level anxiety, a nagging sense that something is missing or unfulfilled in your life? Have you ever felt there was a train you should have boarded but it's too far gone to catch? You are not alone; I've felt these things many times in my life. The resulting anxiety is agitating and agitation seems to deplete our skills, but what is actually fading is our will. Our perceived lack of skills shakes our confidence and inevitably begets indolence.

The problem is that once we recognize our shortcomings and agonize over fixing them, we see a seismic gulf between where we are and where we want to be. We think we need a massive infusion of motivational energy or a lucky break to bridge this gulf. Fortunately, that's not the reality of the situation. The gulf isn't really as big as your perception of it. It's simply a matter of perspective. Crossing it can be a gratifying flight, rather than a scary leap.

You don't feel motivated right now because motivation erodes over time. You start a healthy regimen or begin writing a business plan or research adult education, but as the days go by the distracters take precedence over your whims. Whether it is work, the holidays, the kids, the seasons or the relatives, they all nip away at your desire. You skip the gym one day, then one week, and then jeez, it's been years. You watch a sitcom rather than read a book. Soon the gulf between you and your ideal life begins to widen, until it seems improbable you will ever muster the big steaming pile of energy you would need to bridge it.

We don't notice the ebb of enthusiasm. It is gradual, imperceptible, like the yellowing of our teeth or the expanding of our waistlines. It seems we wake up one day and discover an overweight underachiever staring back from the mirror in disgust. The old Joe is a lifetime gone, never to bound again to higher plains without a major life change that we are too timid, unsettled or dare I say too lazy to undertake. Norman Cousins said, "The great tragedy of life is not death, but what dies within us while we live." The good news however, is that effective, enduring motivation actually begins with making tiny changes in lifestyle. Just as minor adjustments in eating habits lead to sustained weight loss, each small success gives you the confidence to try the next and then the next bigger step.

We've all started projects we didn't complete. Our garages are cluttered with unused exercise equipment, the old car we're refinishing and half-built dog houses. We think these things are what we need to break out of doldrums, but it's not true. We simply need to understand our capabilities, devise a plan and begin to trust our brains. They are amazing little blobs of electro-chemical energy.

You will learn to make minor changes in your daily activities that are designed to get you in the habit of achievement. As you progress through incremental changes like those in your morning routine, you will draw a broader base line of personal development. You will set a higher personal standard. It will actually be harder to revert back to your old ways. Continual improvement becomes part of your character, not just an exhortation from a life coach. Accomplishing small steps and realizing the culmination of a plan have intrinsic rewards. The journey becomes as enjoyable as the final goal. That rising satisfaction is what keeps you moving forward. Motivation then becomes a lifestyle choice, not a mysterious force. You will set small goals out of habit, and then fix your sights on larger, more stimulating objectives.

You're grandest goal should be what Viktor Frankl called "a compelling future vision," but to achieve it you must make a commitment to take those small steps and then continue to build upon them. There are landfills of information about how to psyche yourself up, to motivate and ennoble your wayward soul, but many of the popular sources rev you up with no direction. What inevitably happens is you run into walls, and running into walls hurts, especially if you do it enthusiastically. To sustain directed motivation, you need a flexible tool for developing a plan you can execute, with routes plotted out and benchmarks for assessing your progress. Armed with this plan you will certainly and finally bridge that gulf. You cannot do this with desire alone. This book will teach you the process of formulating the exact plan you need.

Galileo said, "You cannot teach a man everything, you can only help him to find it within himself." Our brain power is self-directed. When a chance to learn presents itself you can choose to absorb the enlightenment or walk away. Look at sources of learning as light switches. Flipping them on doesn't just illuminate the immediate area, but guides you to more switches in more rooms, to more knowledge, and perhaps a deeper existence.

I will teach you a proven system that is all around us, even as you read these words. It is a strategic pathway to the place you aspire to be. It is an opportunity to be responsible for your own exhilaration, a chance to shine over your life and family. I will demonstrate how the emerging science of genetic expression (epigenetics) has all but ruled out heredity as a determining factor in high achievement.

Some of you are seekers. You've taken some risks, worked hard but faltered or experienced self-doubt and for you, the concept of building levels is a better method. It's a directed manner of thinking. You may be motivated, but you need a better map. Motivation without a plan accomplishes nothing. You still aspire, or vaguely remember a time when you did. Many of you have felt your time has passed, that you've let go of your sense of hope. Yet on some level, you still want to be a chef, write a romance novel, open a cigar store, play the clarinet, be a better father, import artesian wine, learn Mandarin, become an aviator, a chiropractor or teach the blind, but lost your way. You think there are no more corners left to turn. You may think you're too old. I've written this book to prove you are wrong. You can develop your expertise in any field you choose and apply your new core competencies to any project you desire.

Why do we care? What's the difference if we just enjoy the moment and survive life? What's with this need to achieve? Does it all really matter?

Well of course it matters. It matters now, and will matter more so tomorrow. If it didn't matter to those who came before us, I wouldn't have the computer with which I wrote this book, or the device on which you're reading it, or the car you drove to renew your gym membership or anything else off an endless list of luxury appointments and facilitating essentials. Do you remember all those people in your life who love you? Well it matters to them. Hey, maybe where you are right now is good enough. Is it? Consider this.

I think 'good enough' is actually an arbitrary term, not defined by an accepted standard but one levied at the point of exhaustion. "That's it; I'm done trying - it's good enough." It's a sign post of rationalization. It's a level beyond which you choose not to excel, rather that one you purposely attained. By finding yourself there you can declare it as intentional.

Blessing our lives as good enough is not an achievement; it's a decision. Once we make the decision to be satisfied we can then practice our repertoire of justifications: I have a roof over my head, I have food in the fridge, the kids aren't in jail, I don't have herpes. The list ebbs and flows through cities and subcultures.

However, we can live extraordinarily on The Seventh Level and set standards of existence that reach out to the unknown. We don't congratulate ourselves for acquiring a lifestyle we arrived at by accident. We push just a little bit more, read just one more book, explore one more idea, add a little more value, reach out to one more person. We look to improve every day. We don't break the streak. We don't carpe diem, we persequi cras (pursue tomorrow). We pursue tomorrow because today was great. Lucius Seneca said, "It is not because things are difficult that we do not dare, it is because we do not dare that they are difficult."

You can say your diet is good enough and that you get enough exercise, but that's because you've forgotten what it's like to feel great. You can say you've seen enough, until one more piece of architecture makes you say, "Jeez would ya look at that." You can say you enjoy being alone, until a friend makes you laugh, or a hug makes you cry.

Yes, it's easy to say, "My life is good enough," and sometimes you do have to wonder if we push too hard, or if we set unreasonable standards. But I don't think so. I don't want to exist. I want to live optimally. Good enough is not one of my goals.

I have a brain with an endless capacity for wonder and learning. My body will serve me well for many more decades if I take care of it. My children, my friends, my professional relationships and my contributions to the world will continue to flourish as I seek to improve. I don't want to wait to die. I can't wait to live.

Cha-Cha-Cha Basic Steps

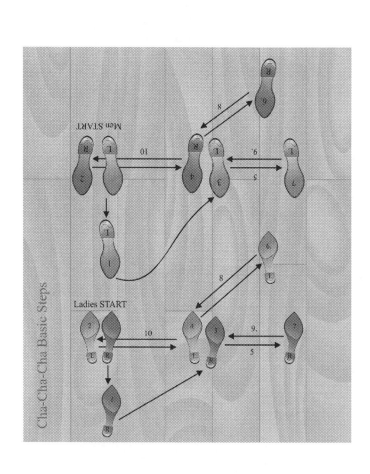

How To Use This Book

This book is inspired by architecture and the big-brained architects who create the built environment. I wrote it for two reasons. The first but lesser motivation is to enlighten humble Joe's like you and me about the interesting but arcane universe in which architects labor. But more importantly I want to help you realize your extraordinary life from the perspective of their ingenuity and their thoughts about how to build something worthwhile.

The premise of this book is a concept; totally centered on the principles of architectural design. I express all references to personal development in relation to architecture, not in the esoteric sense, but with the idea of building something. It's about design, strategy and construction. You have to accept the concept and run with it or the idea just won't work. You have to play along.

This book is not for professional architects. It's about how they work. It's also not for architectural students; they will shape their craft through years of formal schooling and apprenticeships. This book is for the rest of us, those restless souls who feel a need to achieve but don't know where to start. It's is for people like me, the last of a generation, the caboose of the baby-boomer train. It's for those of us mid-prime who know we want to do something challenging in the second half of our lives. We want to matter to our children, to upscale our sense of self-worth, but can't get past this curtain of limiting beliefs to explore our own potential. It's not a text book for design but a play book for you to design a better way for you to live, to let loose whatever it is that's pacing inside.

I was a sheriff's officer for 25 years, eventually attaining the rank of captain, which in that parochial world earned me a modicum of respect.

But I was frustrated with not having the ability to be creative and to share my ideas. I needed to find a way to show people how to accomplish something rewarding, to build something extraordinary.

My interest in architects and their design strategies came upon me inadvertently. While studying geniuses for another project, I read about Filippo Brunelleschi, the Renaissance mastermind who designed, engineered and built the enormous, Il Duomo (The Basilica di Santa Maria del Fiore) in Florence, Italy. I toured the church while on vacation in 1987, but didn't fully appreciate the majesty of the structure because I was preoccupied with a raven-haired, doe-eyed tour guide named Seneta.

Reading about Brunelleschi's life and work intrigued me and so I read about other architects and soon, I was hooked. Their ideas blended perfectly with my thoughts about personal development. I began to see a correlation between architectural design philosophy and human endeavor of all sorts. I believe the wisdom of architects is alluring to those of us who wish to live other-than-average lives because they have systems and a process for generating ideas, developing those ideas into a workable framework, and then executing their plan into something useful and beautiful. It's truly marvelous how it all comes together. But it's not an impossible process. I have broken it down into easily understandable steps so that anyone can master the process and use it in any application. I have injected the capillaries of this book with the relative perceptions of architects in hopes that once you read it, your psyche will be permeated with the kind of thinking that makes their work so fascinating.

This book is intended to create an experience, much as architecture is. Buildings are not simply about their innovative design. They are about experience. You cannot fully appreciate the visceral murmurings of a unique structure unless you walk through it, sensing the space, the light, the materials and the craftsmanship. This book is meant to be read through and then read again, and finally, worked with and used as a guide. It is meant to be beaten up by the time you have designed your extraordinary life. Grab hold of it and read it with enthusiasm.

The introductory chapter explains the reasoning behind my theories and why you should embrace this type of thinking. Skim through Levels One thru Six just to get a sense of where you will be going, an over-arching view of the concept. After you have done that, put the book down for a day. Examine your heart and find your purpose. It's pointless to do this without one. Then clean up your work or study space, get a good chair, put in a fresh light source and get excited. On day two, get paper and pencil ready and begin methodically reading through the entire book. You should be able to read the whole thing in a couple of days. Use a hawks-and-sea-turtles manner of study. Be the hawk first; circle the field and get a good picture of the overall strategy. If you see something of interest; swoop down and take a closer look, then fly back up to scan. When you're finished the first run-through, be a sea turtle. Take a big breath and dive in deep; examine every reef, every cave. Work slowly and patiently, like a forager. It's why they live so long. And please read the appendix about the architects. I have included a short description of each one who is quoted in the text.

Once this phase is done and your restive heart is primed, go back through it and construct your levels. Do not move on to the next level until you have finished shaping the one you're with. Each level, once completed, informs the shape of the next one. Because of this they interlock, creating a stronger overall mission. The method of reading this book is as much a process as the book itself is about process. Working this book is like switching on the high beams in your car. It merely provides a better source of illumination for you to find your own way.

{And please forgive my masculine pronouns. Much of the text is directed in the mirror as well as to you, kind reader. I admire the resilience of women. I have been fortunate to meet some spectacular women during the writing of this book. I simply use the masculine pronouns for ease of writing and consistency.}

As you read this book, try to think in terms of the underlying concept, which is to imagine you and your life as a place, a structure to be designed, adapted, built to last, expanded and cared for over time. It's a place where dreams are accepted and ideas are shared. By thinking of you in terms of place, you must also think about the attendant elements of foundation, systems, perception, context, presentation and interconnectedness; with the natural environment, the community and the people who share that space.

If you are not willing to put in the extra time, then maybe you're not ready to change your life. That's fine, we understand. But if you are committed, then this is a place to start. If you believe in your mission you will generate the ferocious psychology that will drive you to complete it. This book should be a little worn around the edges when you're finished, just like you. You should carry it, write in it, draw on it, stuff notes in it, wrap rubber bands around it and refer to it throughout the process. This is not a hobby. This is worthwhile and requires effort. You are about to begin a true labor of love and this book is a symbol of that effort. Feel free to begin.

Purpose

*"Optimism is what drives architecture forward.
Architecture is the only profession where you have
to believe in the future." - Daniel Libeskind*

The process of architecture is the instrument you will use to design your extraordinary life, but only you can know your purpose. You have your reasons why - you want the new Jag or the custom suits or the 3D home theater. They're all nice, but they're stuff, they're status symbols. Ok, they're meaningless crap. What you really need is purpose.

Purpose is what makes you appreciate the work on the way to the goal. Purpose is pure optimism. Purpose is not just a reason to succeed; it is your reason to give back. It's about bringing someone with you on your quest. There are many ways to exert energy. You can push. You can drive. You can smash through barriers. Much of what is written in personal development is about channeling these types of energy. But there is another kind. There is the energy to lift. The energy to help, to guide, to take someone with you. There is the energy transferred when you reach out, when you create lasting moments.

Think about some of the most significant images from disasters like terror attacks or earthquakes. What always resonates? What images can get even you tough guys to well up? It's the rescuer hoisting the baby from the rubble. It's the story of a man trapped in the World Trade Center who was exhausted and wanted to give up, but a firefighter's hand reached out to him and said, "Not today buddy. You're not dying today. We're getting out of here together. Now stand up - let's go."

That's what purpose does that reasons why can't. Purpose creates moments and life gives them to us all. My children are my purpose. I have been blessed with moments you can only feel, not describe. When my daughter Kaitlin was about two years old she fell asleep on my chest as I sat back on the couch on a quiet Saturday afternoon. The serenity of her trust and comfort eased my mind of all my troubles that day and I fell asleep with her.

We adopted my son Jackson from Vietnam when he was just two months old. The 16 months of anxiety that led to finally holding him for the first time and seeing him look up at me as though he knew and that foreign place became our place, is a moment that is not just unforgettable but is in reality a gift. Purpose then becomes a reason to give your heart, not just a reason to succeed.

Real purpose is about bringing them along with you, teaching and embracing and giving them moments, so they can someday find their own purpose. Purpose is not motivational; it's inspirational. Purpose is not one good thing; it's the only thing.

Purpose is what makes the journey rewarding, so that even if you don't hit your highest aspiration, you have been rewarded by what you've given back. Remember the story of "The Wizard of Oz?" What were the lessons learned? Was the movie just about Dorothy getting home? No - it was about the yellow brick road, the journey, the quest, the finding of heart and courage and the forging of life-long friendships.

Motivation is about reaching down to lift yourself up. Purpose is about reaching out to lift someone else up. Motivation is finally rebuilding that listing garage; purpose is building a tree house with your son.

Purpose is powerful. Whatever it is that this book may help you design; it won't be extraordinary without purpose. Purpose will make the process rewarding, not the goal. When you have purpose; it's enough that you tried. It's enough that you cared. It's enough that you held out your hand. But like my father used to say, "Hey Joe, enough's enough already." So let's build.

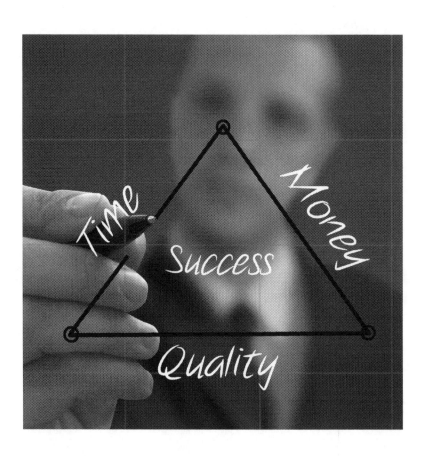

Why Architecture? Why You?

*"Architecture begins to matter when it brings delight
and sadness and perplexity and awe along with
a roof over our head." – Paul Goldberger*

You're still reading so maybe you do have an tingle of aspiration left. You need to achieve but you undoubtedly have many questions. Gratefully, the answer to how you achieve what matters is not shivering in a cave in Tibet or mumbling in the bowels of the Vatican libraries. It's simple and pragmatic.

The solution is rooted in the extensive network of architectural practices. Why architecture? It's not just because architecture is artful, and its artisans idealistic; that's clear enough. But what is overlooked because of its very ubiquity is that architecture is the most pervasive created element of our lives; because architecture is at its core, a process - a thorough, coherent yet impassioned creative process, shaped into a structure of usable art. Architects have systems waiting to be embraced by all of us who need to tap on the door jam of possibility or perhaps, stare at it and then slink away. Get back here chickens.

The quote by Paul Goldberger at the top is apt for the underlying theme of this book. It's about doing the right thing - providing the roof - but doing it in an extraordinary way, in a way that makes us feel alive and to feel that we matter.

We are going to build something together. We will turn your daydreams into ideas, your ideas into concepts and your concepts into reality. You will identify exactly what you want after first identifying your starting points. We'll begin with the source of my inspiration, architecture, and the functional beauty that wraps around our lives each day - comforting, protecting, enticing... without saying a word. We'll lock arms with the architects and use their brain power as a force multiplier. They may not realize it, but they're on our team. You haven't noticed them, but they are with us every day. There is no practical reason to do this alone and sharing, as it turns out, is actually fun. Thanks mom.

But how or where do we begin? It all begins with an idea. We've all had them, even you, I suspect. From the modest small business arrangement to the next Olympic village; ideas spark the striker of your ventures, but ideation drives the enterprise of architecture. Ideation is the action of generating, nurturing, and implementing ideas. It is essential in the cycle of any design process.

The statement "everything begins with an idea" might seem trite, even obvious, irrespective of its truth. However, it's an important component of a forceful process, one of designing that elusive and poorly identified better life. Whether your ideas are evolutionary or revolutionary; commercial, artistic, philosophical or innovative, the stretching of your synapses into an actionable plan to see them accomplished is a skill you can learn and master.

So, how do we progress along higher and higher plateaus? How do we tackle a better-then-mundane endeavor? How do we become the architects of our mission?

We begin by asking questions, lots of them. Then we question the answers we get. Questions are endemic to the architectural mindset. Daniel Libeskind says, "Architecture is the asking of questions. It's not only the giving of answers; it's also like life - the asking of questions." We can begin by asking two questions; why not, and what if. These are flint questions, designed to spark ideas. Together we will discover how asking new questions is the simplest way to discover new ideas. Changing your questions changes your perspective. Changing your perspective leads to new insights. New insights are what we are seeking. They are the tools that configure our thinking mechanism. But we need a little help, an advisor, a team or better yet, experienced mentors. So who will be our mentors?

Why, the architects of course, along with their methods, philosophies, motivations and systems. In the past we've relied on coaches, uncles and other small-town experts for our modest quests, from a better batting average, to juicier cupcakes, to bathroom renovations. And for short-term projects those people were useful. But what happens after you finally conjure up the Big Kahuna of ideas? There won't be room on the couch for you and your formidable friend, so someone will have to move. I joke about 'the couch' sometimes, not to be the Don Rickles of motivation, but because it is a personal metaphor for my lack of productivity. The couch is not a bad place, but it's a bad place for me. It means I'm not working. Maybe I'm a little obsessive but that suits me. You have to find your own methods and run with whatever system works best for you.

It would be ridiculous for me to assume that everyone reading this is fat and lazy; quite the opposite it true. But I've fought laziness my entire life and often my references to that affliction are self-directed. I've developed a sense of humor about it that can be sarcastic, but it's all in good fun. That being said...

Is now an ideal time to blow the dust off your brain and set off in search of accomplishment? The answer to that is always, yes. What do you wish to do; start a business, learn a new subject, play an instrument or are you ready to rejuvenate, resurrect and re-design your life? Just having things isn't enough; we need to feel fulfilled from inside our emotional command post. Beyond having we need to do, to work, to enjoy the cultivation of learning and innovation, of science, art and human exceptionalism. Frank Lloyd Wright said, "A great architect is not made by way of a brain so much as he is made by way of a cultivated enriched heart." This notion of cultivation is significant. Nothing cultivates itself; not a field, a brain, a child, or an idea.

So, improving your bowling average isn't fulfilling anymore? Need a cue for self-actualization? Begin with this concept. In the higher order of designing a better life for ourselves we must first create a lasting, organic process. We need a process that is simple in concept but expandable depending on the demands placed upon it. This is the endowment of the seven level concept. Each level is a component of the plan. The depth of your levels can be as simple or complex as they need to be, but the basic concept is never complicated. Building them creates a process. Everything requires a process, whether it is a minor tweaking of lifestyle or our magnum opus. Swiss architect Le Corbusier said, "All great art is a process," and no group has ever done process better than architects.

I asked an architect out of Chicago, Saaema Alavi, to define architecture for us.

"The definition of Architecture has morphed over the years making the term such a variable these days..."Architecture" can mean:

The art and science of design and erecting buildings and other physical structures.

A general term to describe buildings and other infrastructures.

A style and method of design and construction of buildings and other physical structures.

The practice of an architect, where architecture means to offer or render professional services in connection with the design and construction of a building, or group of buildings and the space within the site surrounding the buildings, that have as their principal purpose human occupancy or use.

Design activity, from the macro-level (urban design, landscape architecture) to the micro-level (construction details and furniture).

The term "architecture" has been adopted to describe the activity of designing any kind of system, and is commonly used in describing information technology."

While some of us are strongly analytical, linear, practical left-brain thinkers, others of us are artistically sensitive, global right brainers. All of us are a little of both. But architects are blessed with effective capacities in both regions, and they work them symbiotically to turn their visions into working structures. Their greatest asset is their ability to translate sensations into steel, mortar, stone, and glass, in order to reinvigorate, create and inspire, with resolve to see their vision erected. They are believers in probability, not possibility, that is until they redefine what's possible.

Architects have a system for blending art and science and creating a lasting achievement. Architects are the great enablers. They build structures that enable us to survive and work. They build spans that enable us to connect cities, islands and cultures. They design museums, art galleries and entertainment spaces like the Sydney Opera House, that enable us to enjoy the swoon of awe. They have a unique capacity to synthesize artistic inspiration and linear thought. No profession so embodies the transitional aptitude for morphing right brain inspiration into left brain oeuvre. This is a chance to learn from the masters of the most enduring process of civilization.

Interestingly, the process is connected to the finished product as the water is to the wet. In fact, architects practice the only art form in which the developmental steps are admired as much as the finished product. Their sketches, models and blueprints are displayed in reverence because they represent what is remarkable about architects, that is, the manner in which they create. Their very thoughts are read by the examiners of their plans, the critics, professors and their students. As their ideas evolve, better methods, inventive solutions and more stunning pictures emerge to enlighten and serve as edification for the next generation.

Their portrayal of life is rendered in their sketches and shaped through their plans. In describing the architectural process, Peter Sackett, from a northwest component of the American Institute of Architects, AIA Seattle said, "In many, if not all, artistic fields, artists are unwilling to allow people to see their work before they have finished. But in this unusual intermediate exposure, a project's awkward stage is celebrated instead of hidden. In this context, therefore, the word 'yet' is not an apology, it is suspense."

In thinking like architects, we develop a style of sharing our evolving ideas with our support structure, our mentors and friends. We instill in ourselves the importance of working the process. It's the process that we will pass on, not the result. Donald Trump has closed countless real estate deals, but his successful book was called, "The Art of the Deal," not "Here's a List of the Properties I Bought." It's safe to assume he's taught his children how to work those deals. That's how you build a legacy.

I suppose I should confess I have a perverse fascination with architects. Not in a stalker kind of way; it's just that I am captivated with their high-function brains and the breadth of their ability to create purposeful art. As the great 'solutionists', architects unwittingly teach us that we can solve all manner of design problems, whether for a business, a personal objective or the creation of a new self.

Does it matter? Yes, because architecture itself matters. I.M. Pei said, "Architecture is the very mirror of life. You only have to cast your eyes on buildings to feel the presence of the past, the spirit of a place; they are the reflection of society."

Architecture can stir the excitement of running into a stadium, the trepidation of our first day at school, the dread that Dan Ariely might feel in a hospital or the serenity of a chapel. It can strike romantic or fearful chords, resonating as an integral part of our own stories. Without architecture, our memories would be set on empty stages.

When does it matter? How will it pertain to the designing of our extraordinary lives? According to architecture critic Paul Goldberger, "It (architecture) matters when it goes beyond protecting us from the elements…architecture happens when people build with an awareness that they are doing something that reaches at least a little bit beyond the practical."

In correlation, our endeavors matter when they are undertaken for the sake of making something uncommon, or achieving a better existence, something to look back upon with a smile. It's what happens to us non-architects when we dare to attempt things in our lives that are exciting, or at least a little bit beyond boring. Hey, sometimes boring is good. We can count on boring to always be there.

But boring is also, well, boring and many of us stare in rapt envy across the moat of tedium. Some of us feel an impulse to create, to build, to flourish or simply to live optimally, hoping that when we are being yanked down the hall to that last long light that we at least gave a few things a shot, we pushed for maximum output.

OK so architecture is important, but what makes the architects so special?

According to the web site of the American Institute of Architects, the AIA, "Architects are conceivers of structures. They are creative, analytical, curious, imaginative, artistic and mathematical. They are at ease with the creative process, not intimidated by it. They are unique in the artistic world in that they are not only proud but eager to show their work before it is completed. Their plans and drawings, art in themselves, are an important part of the finished work. The ideation, the working of ideas, is the character of the structure. Without it the building has no persona. It is merely protection from the rain.

Architecture blends art and science to create places where people live, work, play, learn, worship, meet, govern, shop and travel: public spaces and private places; indoors and outdoors, on land, sea and sky; in neighborhoods, towns, suburbs and cities.

Architecture is a passion, a mission, a calling – a career."

So, what am I getting at here?

Since architecture is so pervasive, it is a natural progression of thought to suggest that the architectural design process would apply to designing our extraordinary life, in parallel with a basic architectural algorithm. Everything architecture represents and nearly all that architects have done for millennia continue to touch civilization in so many ways that we can honor their process by using it to design our ventures. I hope just by reading this book, you are feeling the rage to achieve, but as Peter Sackett says, "…to disregard the rich process by which an idea becomes a place is to miss most of the story. At the end we may know the facts, but not why they matter." Similarly, our own projects are enriched by working through and savoring the process by which we accomplished them.

This is the continuum. Architecture matters because it is where we achieve. Architects matter because they have developed the best processes for building those places. Our endeavors matter because why we need to accomplish them matters to our families, loved ones and our own prosperity. This book it is about how to use the best system, developed by the best planners, to accomplish our most important goals.

Paul Goldberger, in describing his boyhood yearnings of New York City, said the cityscape was "one vast, complicated, enticing object, full of peaks and valleys and nooks and crannies, but one big, interlocking thing, a product of nature like Yellowstone or Yosemite as much as a serendipitous collection of man-made elements."

Doesn't this sound an awful lot like a description of life? Some things are natural, genetic and earthly, while others are made by us, of our own volition; our decisions, impulses and derring-do's. Architectural processes are actually a part of our lives already. Their basic methods are easily adopted by us to design our life plans; they are natural to us. The concept of this book is simple; to demonstrate how the fundamentals of the architectural process can be drawn upon to direct us through to the satisfying completion of countless activities. So it's not just about collecting a bunch analogies to architecture. It is about replicating a proven process which has been worked and lived in each day for all manner of labor, leisure and trade.

Architecture is about solving problems, so why not take advantage of this mindset to solve our life design problems? Not convinced yet? This is a process that earns international acclaim.

The architectural community annually honors its own with the esteemed Pritzker Prize. It was started in 1978 by the fabulously wealthy Pritzker family. It has been called the Nobel Prize of architecture, architecture's Pulitzer, the MVP of CAD (architects will find that amusing). The Hyatt Foundation, sponsors of the Pritzker Prize, describe the spirit of the award, "To honor a living architect whose built work demonstrates a combination of those qualities of talent, and commitment, which has produced consistent and significant contributions to humanity and the built environment through the art of architecture."

How architects work will reveal itself to you as you build your levels. Patrick Nuttgens stated, "In the final analysis, all architecture reveals the application of human ingenuity to the satisfaction of human needs." As our needs seem to be endless, so are the imaginative ways in which architects satiate them. Their way they solve problems is grounded in 'best practices' developed through the amalgam of thousands of years of visionary application. The neat thing is, this process has always been available to us regular folks; we just haven't noticed. That's my job.

From Angkor Wat in Cambodia to the Imperial Hotel in Tokyo, across to the Eltz Castle of Austria and the Allen Lambert Galleria in Toronto, architecture has preceded our lives and will be the archeology of our progeny. But no matter how dramatically architecture has changed throughout time and across cultures, no matter which philosophy or style has reigned, from pyramids to brownstones, the original energy took shape in the mind of man. Ideas precede all art, whether it is the kind we stare at – sometimes perplexed – or the kind we live in.

I developed the premise of this book by deconstructing the process of architectural development. Architects do the same thing, that is, they begin with the end in mind. They have a general idea, a lean vision of a finished structure, and then they go back and figure out how to build it. Along the way the vision changes subtly, twists this way or shades to another, but stays true to the original idea. This book will help you build the seven levels needed to complete your life design.

The Levels

You have heard the conventional metaphor of construction before, but I think it's gone under-explored. Many trainers have told us that in order to build something excellent, we need to begin with a solid foundation. Although the metaphor was understandable and useful, I continued to question it. You certainly can't just show up at an empty lot and start digging a foundation. How wide should it be? How deep? How many workers and machines, of what type? Don't you need permits and contracts for this sort of thing?

And more importantly, you need a plan. You need engineers, builders, contracts, soil evaluation, site surveys, financing and a host of other prerequisites. I wondered what else you needed; so I started asking questions.

Before the foundation, you need to work out an exhaustive array of details, commonly known as the blueprints. Before the blueprints there must be a decision-making process involving designers, artists, engineers and the client. During this phase the preliminary (presentation) plans or prototypes are drawn, painted or modeled and then presented to clients. Sometimes they are presented to panels of judges for architectural competitions. This gives the clients or judges something real to look at, a visual representation of the design so they can make changes and determine if it is feasible, given the physical dimensions, lay of the land, political issues and financial constraints. This phase is the second of seven essential components.

The first phase rests in the anointed mind of the architect. It begins with an concept, born in the right half of the brain in a swirl of color, experience, sound and enigma. Some people have a natural ability to tap these skill sets and some of us, most of us, need guidance and simple methods. The first of your seven levels is a fun and interesting way to tap your natural ingenuity. It will help you decide upon the one thing that you always wanted for your life. It's in the exploration of this first level that you will jump-start the confidence you need to attain your vision.

Let's review and move forward.

Building your levels is about asking questions and solving problems. Architects solve problems for a living: problems of design, structure, balance and aesthetics. We all love to look at the urbane work architects produce, but what really fascinates me is the how. The way they work

25

from ideas back to structure intrigues me. It's almost a reverse solution search, always underpinned by the image of the finished product.

Level One. The architect's ideas are first brought to life by a rough sketch written down on anything available at the moment of inspiration. In my case it would be a bar nap. After this, they fabricate the more formal renditions of the concept which includes a final decision about the scope of the project (Level Two). Eventually they work with the engineers to produce the plans (Level Three).

Only after they complete the first three phases can they finally unchain the big-boy tools and start digging the foundation. This is your Fourth Level, your bedrock. It is a time to set your working persona and express your core beliefs. It's a time for honest self-reflection. Your identity is the unconscious force behind your decisions. Once the foundation is set, you will begin the real construction work.

Level Five is the biggest and most production-oriented platform. It is your due diligence phase, the structural vertebrae of the building as well as your life design. This is where the iron-workers play. To build Level Five you will complete the background development and set up shop, write your book, finish your schooling or licensing requirements.

But before the building can be finished there must be systems put in place to sustain it. These are vital to the life of the building, literally not just figuratively. This important segment is represented in Level Six as our habits of achievement. It's what we do each day to sustain and improve upon the better life we've built through Levels Four and Five.

Level Seven is where you are fulfilled. It's the finished product. This is the plants in the offices, the art on the walls, the polishing of the granite, the culmination of well-born decisions. But this level is as much about review as it is rejoicing. You need to review your process, develop best practices, pass on your lessons learned and congratulate yourself on a job well conceived and well worked.

This is a time to be proud and share your experience. And as long as you've put systems in place to sustain what you have created, you can enjoy it for the rest of your days. You will have stretched to new-found skills, those that will help you envision even further. It all looks like this:

Phase	Architectural Process	Level	Life Design
1	Concept or vision, rough sketch	1	Ideas, thoughts, wishes, dreams and desire. To what do I aspire?
2	Detailed sketch, rendition, design style, model, drawing	2	Form, focus, substance, precision, designation, clarity of purpose, decisions.
3	Blueprints and other design and/or systems plans	3	Detailed action plan, direction, rudder, decisions, enlisting of support resources.
4	Foundation, clearing the rubble	4	Character Change, self-questions, identity, purpose, parti.
5	Frame, steel, structural core, rivets, welds and iron (the bones)	5	Due diligence, the dominant work of the project
6	Functional operating systems, electric, plumbing, HVAC, fiber optics, maintenance systems	6	Habits – Life Systems, that which sustains the plan, persistence, expertise, mastery.
7	Finish work, art, façade, color, glass, furniture, the human element, review, best practices	7	Pinnacle, fulfillment, review, mentoring, accomplishment, lessons learned, reward & reflection.

Ludwig Mies van der Rohe said, "Architecture begins when you place two bricks carefully together." The architecture of endeavor begins when you look an idea in the eye. It begins when you imagine the rush of action, not the mere possibility of daydreams. It takes hold when you accept this essential premise; you can build the best version of you using the architectural process as a tool. It is a tool used by some of the most creative and resourceful minds of history. It's been used by ancient civilizations, before the age of bronze when they were still using rocks for hammers. Their tool belts must have been bulky. The best and the brightest of planning and design have used it so why not us? Why not you? The architectural process can be complex, but in elementary terms it is easily applied to solving the problems that have held you back from personal achievement.

So...Why you? Why now?

Who are you to presume you can create, that you are bold enough to work with the timeless system used in the forming of the built world; a system used by the ingenious Leonardo da Vinci, the pioneering Mies van der Rohe, the monumental Louis Kahn? Who are you to imagine that you can capture your vague notions of prosperity or your ambiguous life refurbishings and give them a full composition you can achieve through a simple formula? (explosions and swelling music) Who are you mere trundlers who would put yourselves in the company of genius?

Well I will put you there. You deserve it. This is a company of achievers with whom you belong, so long as you make a commitment to work the chapters of this book, to shape each of your seven levels in progression. You must accede to the proven system of structure that is forged through ideation and honest work. You must be willing to stretch your imagination and your abilities. In the end you will be proud. Nothing worthwhile is easy. This will require work and commitment. The difference between what you've tried before and what you will accomplish now is the impetus for change, the need to show off the process. To help you understand this strategy it is useful to understand an aspect of the human condition. Abraham Mazlow taught us we cannot move on to self-actualization without first being satisfied and comfortable within the realm of the social and psychological needs. The needs to belong, to aspire, to create and to leave a lasting impression, are all met by the building of your seven levels. You don't need to be a genius, just driven. "Genius is talent set on fire by courage." - Henry Jackson Van Dyke

So let's roll up our sleeves, lighten up, have fun and build something really cool. You haven't missed all the trains yet. A big-city train station is a convergence of many lines, some good, some poor, like so many decisions. Some lead you away from loss, others in the direction of gain. When the engine bellows and a train rolls out, some of us focus on the leaving, some focus on the destination. Level Sevens focus on the journey. This time we are the engineers. This is the fun part where we get to create lasting impressions. The most important concept to remember from this book is that it is the process that's important. It's why I love architecture. The process becomes the lessons learned and the legacy. The process is a gift.

Working it builds productive behavior patterns. Some of our unproductive patterns that have pulled us in the wrong direction. In the past we have expected to fail, but not any more. Studies of college students have concluded that those with higher expectations of their professors get more from the class. Navy SEALS rehearse victory. Athletes visualize triumph. You can expect success in this new mission, because you will have prepared and planned for it. Professor Dan Ariely concludes, "Expectations can influence nearly every aspect in one's life." You deserve success, so start expecting it.

Level One
Room for Ideas

"The great thing about being an architect is you can walk into your dreams." – Harold E. Wagoner

The idea room is where it all begins. Stand in wonder before your first level, the starting point to a life less ordinary. How does it feel to be in the place where visions take shape? For most of your adult life you have wanted to do something, but didn't know how to begin. So start by changing your frame of reference. Since this book is a big fat homage to architecture, let's build something marvelous. In an interview with ArchDaily.com, Eugene Kohn of KPF Architecture spoke about what goes on inside of buildings. "Our goal as architects is to create buildings that inspire people to do whatever it is in that space they need to do. That inspiration comes from within the building as much as from the way it looks from the outside." If you imagine your starting point as a functioning place, you can see it as a base of operations for ideas. This is really what the idea room represents.

The idea room is a place to search for what you need to start your mission, a workshop for your ideas to take shape. Like Tesla's laboratory, it's a place to let the sparks fly. It's a numinous haven with direct access to stored ideas, windows open to every angle, unopened doors and secret desires. It is a place for you to work on your operating systems, your methodology of thought, emotional introspection; a place to find guidance and courage. Within the idea room you can solicit mentors and collaborate with friends.

It's your place now. Own it. Relish it. Believe in it. "A place belongs forever to whoever claims it hardest, remembers it most obsessively, wrenches it from itself, shapes it, renders it, loves it so radically that he remakes it in his own image." - Joan Didion.

Level One is where you determine your direction, a survey of your talents, resources and aspirations. Architecture is a reflective art form. The architect thinks of design in the aesthetic sense as well as the impact of the particular design. The architecture must respectfully represent and make peace with the physical place while artfully transforming the metaphysical sensations of experience, space and light. Every architectural work, from lofts in Chicago to cityscapes in Nanjing, begins with an idea. In terms of process; the idea is the first working element of architecture.

Architects have a sort of poetic idiom to their language. In his book, "Idea and Phenomena", Steven Holl describes the 'getting started' in perfect architect-speak, "In each project we begin with information and disorder, confusion of purpose, program ambiguity, an infinity of materials and forms. All of these elements, like obfuscating smoke, swirl in a nervous atmosphere. Architecture is a result of acting on this indeterminacy.

To open architecture to questions of perception, we must suspend disbelief, disengage the rational half of the mind, and simply play and explore. Reason and skepticism must yield to a horizon of discovery. Doctrines cannot be trusted in this laboratory. Intuition is our muse. The creative spirit must be followed with happy abandon. A time of research precedes synthesis."

From your idea room you will work to accomplish two things: generate a great idea (Levels 1 & 2) and explore ways to make it feasible (Level 3). It will help in your search for an idea to understand the reasons behind them.

You may feel a restlessness, a need to achieve, an irksome sense that something is missing. You might be wrestling with thoughts of inadequate professional enlightenment. We have all felt this sense of hollowness when we start asking Alfie what it's all about, and since nature abhors a vacuum, we consciously and unconsciously seek to fill the void. We get temporary satisfaction from spending money on junk we don't need or partying but they don't satiate us on an abiding level. What's driving you in these random but short-lived surges of activity? By focusing on what may be missing we can build something other than a headstone at the end of our rut.

Architects don't just generate ideas for no reason. There is a client to suit or a competition to win. Certainly they have a bank of potential design images, their 'someday' watercolors that appear on cerebral sketchpads, but they have one slight advantage over us on their idea platforms; the client or competition gives them a jumping off point. It may be broad in scope or imprecise, but it's something: a museum, a residence, a gymnasium, an office complex or a town square. They may have nothing more to go on but a phrase or a term of purpose, yet they begin.

Your idea room needs a few jumping off points as well. Your jump-point is your 'why'. It's not the same as purpose; we've already discussed that force. Your 'why' is this thing you feel you need to do or a specific objective you need to accomplish.

What is aching, missing, unfinished, unresolved or underutilized? Do you simply need money for a new home, a college bill or a swell car? Do you want to leave a legacy? Do you need to change professions, start a non-profit organization, open a business or finally feel fulfilled on a personal level? Your answers to these questions will be your jump-points. It is from those points that you will generate ideas.

The road from your bland existence into the architectural setting is an exploration of the natural curiosity we are endowed with. Color, form, space, light, emotion and texture become pathways to enlightenment. Architects are comfortable in the creative realm in part because it is inherent to their make-up, but also because they are prepared to be there. They learned some creativity skills during their formal education, but developed them out of a need to solve challenges, such as those presented by engineering or when striking a balance between style and utility. They have learned how simple shapes are starting points for complex structures. They have practiced the fundamentals and thus acquired the expertise that gives them the backbone to try new challenges.

Anthony Garetti, an award-winning producer of television commercials, told me he's become more creative because of the time he spends studying other creative people in his field. He has literally watched thousands of hours of films which have helped to build an intricate platform for his own ideas. Ideas in motion are Garetti's business just as buildings are the business of architects. Each profession has jump-points, and you must identify yours, which is the reason that homing in on your 'why' is so important.

Wonder

"Architecture is not based on concrete and steel and the elements of the soil. It is based on wonder." - Daniel Libeskind.

Seeing what other don't, asking what others won't, deflecting limitations, seeking rather than accepting, and scrutinizing your most compelling aspiration; these are some of the thought processes that are used as tools for shaping your first stone. Question everything, not just to be contrary, but to be curious. Welcome radical ideas. Andy Rooney always asked, "Did you ever wonder why...?"

Embrace your capacity to wonder. One of my favorite quotations from Einstein is, "He who can no longer pause to wonder, and stand rapt in awe, is as good as dead; his eyes are closed."

Revisit the unencumbered brain of your childhood. When my son Jack let go of his balloon on a soggy September morning and we watched it rise high into a sycamore tree, I knew it was a goner. Jack wondered if maybe a friendly pterodactyl could come by and pick him up to go fetch it. Well why not? A child wonders because he has no references or anchors. (Anchors in this cognitive sense would be his first understanding of any concept; afterwards, all other meanings ascribed to this thing would be compared to his first learning of it). He has no parameters, so he has no limitations on what he may ask about. He hasn't yet learned to feel silly that he may be asking a dumb question. He is not embarrassed about his lack of understanding. He hasn't acquired enough knowledge to help him relate new concepts to those already confirmed, in order to understand this new thing before him. He doesn't judge his ignorance; he satisfies it.

We learn by building associations. However, our grown-up brains are cluttered with misinformed references and unfortunately we've come to accept them as the right answers. It's what cognitive science calls the primacy effect; that which is learned first is learned best. Most of the time, we don't even know why we know something, we just do. But a child doesn't 'just know' yet, so he continues to ask questions. We didn't need cognitive scientists to tell us this. Socrates said, "Wisdom begins in wonder."

So Jack asks why, a lot. He asks where did it come from and why. He asks who did it and why. He wants to know why I do things. This is how he establishes patterns and begins to build his network of knowledge. When we lose our innate sense of wonder, we diminish our capacity to learn new ideas.

When Frank Lloyd Wright said, "Freedom is from within," he spoke to the concept of self-directed competence. Each of us has access to opportunity and the potential to direct our own success, so we can enjoy the freedom of professional, personal and financial abundance. The harder you work on personal development, the more choices you create. Personal development is like currency; it doesn't buy happiness, but it can give you options. The real freedom comes from recognizing your own talents and using them unconstrained by self-imposed limitations. They are not permanent limits as you may have previously thought but problems to be solved.

Architects are problem solvers. In the pursuit of solutions they are inventive and imaginative. They funnel their education and experience into ingenious ideas. The first of your seven levels and by comparison, the architectural process, is a wholly right-brained, creative escapade; one of sensation and emotion. It is the level of distinctive concepts, exploration, mystery and ingenuity. It's about new vistas and a forward thinking.

The architect's vision is one of either genesis or resurrection. They may be presented with a blank space to fill, or they may stand before a neighborhood rife with decay, but see rebirth. They see what we don't, but we can develop the habits of thinking on a grander scale. In the elegant words of Antoine de Saint-Exupery, "A rock pile ceases to be a rock pile the moment a single man contemplates it, bearing within him, the image of a cathedral."

What is your image? What's your story? What do you see in the rock pile of your ordinary life? Thoughts are free; have as many as you want.

Some of us see decay or rubble as depressing or an excuse to ask, "Why bother?" Architects see neglect as an impetus for change. They see what could yet be not what should have been. They see opportunity, not a reason to judge. They work on a variety of landscapes from empty lots to blank paper, from neglected homes to forgotten waterfronts. Every space is a beginning regardless of what does or does not occupy it.

This is a chapter about getting started. It's about letting go and letting creativity happen. It's about refocusing old ideas and generating new ones. But what if all the great ideas are taken? Do new ideas have a place in your life? That's an odd question.

Maybe you are looking afar for something you haven't yet imagined, even though your unrealized ideas are right here. David Chipperfield, who speaks with the serenity of confidence says, "I think that often people are looking beyond the horizon for something which sometimes is right in from of them. I think in architecture I've always learned; do what's in front of you. It's somehow giving it importance and taking it seriously. It's a good way of approaching architecture." And it's also a good way of approaching this misguided idea that you must do something of world renown to feel a sense of accomplishment. This book is about being extraordinary, a little beyond ordinary, and ordinary is right in front of you, waiting for your stamp to make it your own and leave it better than you found it.

A vision has two core elements. One is creativity and the other is specificity. An entrepreneur named Joe Gentle once told me that most people don't get anything out of life because they don't want anything. "Uh..." I answered profoundly, "What?"

Then I composed myself and said, "Of course people want things. They want stuff, a better life, and buckets of money." He responded by pointing out that my answer was exactly what he was referring to. People say they have desires, but they express them in vague terms, such as "stuff" and "a better life." They don't decide on exactly what they want so they never figure out how to go about acquiring it. They lack focus which means they lack direction which means they can't develop a plan which means they always fail in their half-hearted attempts to improve some aspect of their lives in hopes that it will reveal a more clearly defined outlook on where they are headed.

We make decisions to take one path over another or none at all. Our decisions will define our future. But in order make those decisions; we must know what our options are.

How do you know what your options are? How do you choose one path over another? Where do you want to be in three months, one year or five years? Where and how do you begin?

Anthony Garetti works with all sorts of imaginative people in making television commercials. He says that sometimes you have to test a variety of ideas before you settle on one you like, but the important thing is personal triumph is, "to try and do something you've never done before, whether it's gardening or working with clay or theater or any number of pursuits. You may try a lot of different things over a long period of time before suddenly realizing, 'Hey, I like to paint.' It may take some time but, so what? Whatever it is; it doesn't matter, just do something now, something different, something that stretches you."

What do you love to do? What jacks you up? What, besides a drill sergeant, can get you out of bed at 0530 on a Saturday? What is unfinished or shortchanged? Are you starting something new, like a franchise or a career? Are you learning to play an instrument? Are you seeking optimal performance? Are you working to become a social entrepreneur or save Atlantic sea turtles?

Or is this a renewal? Are you regenerating? Are you beginning a new life or rebuilding a tattered one? Yes, architects see living experiences in empty spaces, but they also have a mindset that differs from the insular outlook of those who merely sit on the porch and watch what happens. One of my mentors, Eric Worre, calls such people tourists. He says, "You can either make things happen or you can be a tourist and wonder what happened."

I am no genius, but I can ponder. I can imagine. I can carry a journal and I can record my thoughts and so can you. Let's all start by overcoming our fear of where our own brains might lead us. You may not be Benjamin Franklin, but you have astounding potential. You don't have to solve world hunger, cure diphtheria or discover the North Pole; we already know where it is. But you simply want to feel that you contributed, (don't you?) that you accomplished something a little special, that you actually acted upon an idea. One small victory will inspire you to try another. Just do something.

Let's say you want to be a chef, but you're obligated to that stifling clerical job. Try this. Get up for a week at 3:30 in the morning and drive to a fish or produce market. Learn how the other chefs pick produce for the day, every day. What kind of fish is that? Where does it come from? How is it cut, stored, served and paired? Which vegetables are best in particular seasons? How much do you order at one time? How is it packaged? How do you set prices? How do you haggle? This is an educational experience you can create for yourself at almost no cost, to test the waters and see if this life really is for you. If just being there - cold, hungry and tired - still has you fired up, then maybe this life is for you. Maybe you should start planning.

Architects turn ideas into a functional reality. Thoughts are biologically and neurologically complex things. We should respect the science of that fact. Our ideas are how we give meaning to visceral experiences and emotions, the desires and obligations of our preconscious souls. Doug Patt says, "Architects make what accommodates who we are." Your life designed as a place will accommodate who you are.

Where do ideas come from? Some of your ideas uncoil from the energy of emotionally charged motives, such as love, family concerns, social responsibility or exuberance. Some come from self-sacrifice for idealism. Some have been planted there long ago. Your thoughts may be instigated by an advertising spot or a story that lingers in your subconscious. Some arise out of need or utility, like an invention. Some just seem fun.

Your sensibility is littered with ideas and even though most of them skip in and out of your consciousness, they somehow remain stuffed away in the dusty corners of your skull. It's understanding how or why you classify those ideas: good, bad, ambivalent, ridiculous, ingenious, awful or frightening, which helps you to find them.

So how do you find these thoughts? How will you figure out precisely what it is you want? How will you make the transition from foggy to fabulous?

Creativity can be developed, much as any skill, through understanding and practice. Part of understanding it comes from the allaying of fears. Most of us can't or won't try anything creative because we don't see ourselves as creative people; we fear that we may look foolish or be mocked. But as überlegen architect Frank Gehry stated, "You've got to bumble forward into the unknown."

We can't all be creative geniuses; that wouldn't be fun. It's why we marvel at them. Some people seem to have endless corridors of imagination, dashing from one bright space to another like titanium butterflies, but you too can be creative in generating workable ideas; you simply have to try a few simple methods. As you work through the exercises, ideas will germinate. Write them down, scribble or roughly sketch them out and tape them on the wall, then keep moving.

This is not about creativity in the sense of designing a building or sculpture; it's about learning to be imaginative so you can figure out what it is you need to do in order to make your life a little bit, just a little bit, better than ordinary. You are working your natural inventor skills to help you define a purpose. Once you begin to express your creative genes, you will mystify your friends. You can finally hear, "That was your idea? Holy Toledo!"

The First Technique: The Brain Safari

Toss some boots and khakis on your brain and take it to unexplored territory. Go ahead, really. A Komodo dragon won't eat it. The Brain Safari is a fun excursion that helps you channel your inner Vasco da Gama while learning to be detail oriented. "Do just once what others say you can't do and you will never pay attention to their limitations again."
- Captain James Cook

The Brain Safari is a kind of directed meditation. It's a conscious dreaming in which all realities are possible, but all decisions are yours, even those made by the unconscious. This type of activity has been shown to produce a theta wave state, which is optimal for pumping out ideas. I have often gotten good ideas while driving long distances on the highway, particularly on a familiar route. I suddenly realize I cannot remember the last 10 or 15 miles, yet I have figured out a solution to a nagging problem. I can travel a highway with little conscious thought, freeing my brain to do other things, like think. The rhythmic droning of Buddhist chants has been shown to produce this theta wave state, and a deeper level of consciousness. It takes practice to become adept at staying focused in your imaginary world, so don't rush it. Picture a novice monk sitting on a cold rock high in the Himalayas with nothing but a couple of crackers and a half cup of yak milk to get him through the day. That's patience.

In order to properly trek, you must find a place to explore, any place that is different from where you are now, then concentrate on really being there. Pretend you just awoke there.

Carefully but aggressively look around in every direction. A broad sweep is not enough. You must look north, south, left, right, up, down, around, behind, through, over and in between. This is a virtual reality immersion in whatever random site you happen on. Pick an unusual place you've never been. If you pick a forest, get yourself deep in the Ural Mountains. If you pick a coastline, make it in a remote corner of the world like Vietnam or Chile. This is a time to be Indiana Jones. After you get good at this you will look for specific items or answers, but in the early stages, just let your searcher loose. Open your socio-archeologist heart and let in whatever you happen upon. Accept the gift of uncertainty. Don't forget to ask questions along the way.

You need to be alone, free to think any way you wish and will need at least 15-20 minutes of that solitude in the beginning. You can eventually work your way into longer sessions of 30-45 minutes. Darken the room a little, but not completely. Put on some soft, instrumental music like nature sounds, a nocturne, an adagio or anything that is soft enough to be non-distracting but just loud enough to block out background noises. I like Jean Sibelius, Maurice Ravel, Claude Debussy and Samuel Barber. Their music stirs images for me. Sit in a comfortable chair and relax. Breathe easily, deeply and quietly. Each place you visit comes with questions. By asking questions you will develop a taste for curiosity.

Where is this remote coastline and how did you get here? Which hemisphere of the world is it in? What type of earth is under your feet; sand, clay or rock? Are the waters calm or are the waves pounding? What are you wearing? Is there a breeze or wind? Is it warming or cooling? Are there people around? Why or why not? What's behind that boulder? How did this clay pot get here? Is it handmade? What's the temperature of the water?

Look toward the water. Which direction is west, across the land or out to sea? How far can you see? Are there outcroppings or vessels on the water? How far out?

Describe them. Notice how you feel. Real imagination is visceral, not simply cognitive. Ask your own questions. No one can hear you. Let go and get after it. This is important.

What time of day or night is it? Are you hungry, thirsty, feisty, calm or nervous? Is there grass or any other vegetation behind you?

Walk toward it. Are you moving uphill? What or who is over the crest of that hill? There is a path in the high vegetation. It's dark, but you must take it. Where is it leading? How does it smell? Can you still hear the ocean? What else do you hear - birds, music, voices, silence? Are you frightened or thrilled? How long will you walk this path? Where is it leading? Wait, you see a light around the bend. There is a change of scenery up ahead. Is it barren, busy or something in between? Are there structures there? What kind? How old are they? Are they in disrepair?

Describe them in detail. Leave nothing out. Walk around behind them, walk through them or fly over them. Why not? Did you find a stranger or a friend just over that broken wall? What did they say to you? What's the condition of the structures? Is there something familiar about them? Will you leave that place or escape? Can you find your way back to the water? Do you care to?

When the session is over take a break, take a walk. Get up and change spots. Just move. Take note of the emotions you may be feeling. Let it work into your subconscious. Take a quick break, then sit down and write everything you can remember in your journal, especially that which surprised you. It's important to write it down immediately or you will forget the details. Tomorrow we walk again.

The Brain Safari works only if you believe in it. You have to let go and immerse yourself. The powerful memories we have are complete in all sensory aspects. I remember the day my father sat down on the toilet, put his hands on my shoulders and told me he was dying. 43 years later I can describe that bathroom in minute detail, including all the colors, smells and obvious emotions. To be creative you must incorporate all your senses so they can trigger hidden ideas and subconscious desires or fears. If a person appears unexpectedly on a safari, engage them, or at least stop and observe them. They can't see you; it's your imagination at work. Let in unfold. Watch them; don't just walk on by. You will be startled by what you discover as you get proficient at this.

Day two: imagine being outside a soaring castle on an improbable granite cliff. (For this exercise, find a free video website and play "The Tempest" by Jean Sibelius - you will be inspired.)

Is the castle immense? How many men built it, over how many years? Does it show signs of age? How can you get inside? Will you climb the walls or slip in through a secret passage? Who lives there? Are you a welcomed visitor? How does it feel in there? Is it cold, damp, surprisingly warm and dry, or musty? What do you sense? What can you hear? Are you in another era? Is something stirring or is it time for vespers? Open doors. Are they heavy, dense, noisy and dark? Can you see clearly or is it a struggle? Are your senses heightened? Have you eaten and do you smell food? Find the kitchen, smell the wood fire, listen to the clank of the plates, the murmur of busy voices. Crawl into the rafters and look down. Make yourself small; make yourself invisible. Move from the kitchen to the war room. Wow, so this is where they keep the crossbows, the arrows and sharpening stones. This is where the fear of battle precedes the smell of death. Touch a sword. What is the handle made of? Pick it up and feel the weight. Hold it over your head. Someone's coming!

By now, you get the idea, so... Where will you go next? What will you find? Who will you meet? Will you engage them in conversation? Are they wise or amazingly foolish, evil or comical? Are they famous, infamous or bit players in a grander scheme? What secrets will they reveal about you? What inspiration will they become for you?

The important thing to remember in your exploration is to take in all the elements. Leave nothing untouched. Notice size, dimension, perspective, sights, sounds, smells, weight, texture, emotion, color, depth, sensations and atmosphere. If you don't notice anything, keep moving. Try another place, another time, another version of you or your viewpoint. Touch things to feel their gravity, their craftsmanship, their skin, their purpose. Are these things as you would expect or are you surprised, confused or maddened? Is the experience invigorating, cathartic, educational, scary, revealing or bland? Did you laugh, cry, brace up or retreat? Did you have a headache afterward or feel as though you needed a drink? Are you excited at your discovery? Did you encounter anyone, from your distant past or near future? Did they speak? Did you answer? Were any old or gnawing questions answered? Write down as much as you can remember and include your feelings about what you found, no matter how bizarre it seems. Put your thoughts in your journal while they are still fresh.

Think about where you'd like to go next. Try a few locations, some large and open like the plains and some small and personal like your childhood home or the school where a famous figure learned to read. Be wacky; who cares? Assume nothing. Preconceive nothing. Do it a few times until you get the hang of looking for details and trying new outlooks. Have fun with the moments you create.

We remember moments, not things. Richard Restak explained the function of the brain in is book, "Mozart's Brain and the Fighter Pilot." He said our brains remember whole experiences, which are tied with emotion, more profoundly than we might remember a list of groceries. Our brains combine different sensory input to create whole experiences. For example, our brains don't separately remember toast, eggs, coffee and a scone; we remember breakfast. Think of an early terrific memory like your first real kiss or the first time someone said, "I love you." If you linger in the moment, you will begin to recall sights, smells, textures, feelings and sounds. The combination of all these features is what led to the permanent placement of that event in your mind.

The lesson is, when you are trying to be creative you should incorporate all the senses. Consider the image in total. If you think of a rock you must imagine how heavy it is, its shape and surface texture. If you think of a storefront you must imagine its location, height, image, level of activity or distance from the street and the type of neighborhood it's in. When you imagine a boardroom full of your personal advisors, you should include the chairs, the aroma of the coffee, the light from the windows, the height of the office space, the floor it occupies, the mood, the ambience and color of the walls or carpet. We are sentient beings and our strongest memories are formed when emotion is interlaced with circumstances and senses. Powerful images touch off our emotional switches and our innate response mechanisms, creating longer-lasting memories. Use every aspect of your brain to develop visions with meaning.

The next step is to think about specific ideas before you go on another safari. Focus on what you like, what excites you, what you have fun with. Ask yourself some questions. What would you love to be doing if there were no distractions, if there were no financial constraints or if time, ability and motivation were not issues? What problem have you been struggling with that you can't seem to resolve? Write everything down. During your next brain safari, your subconscious will help you look for specific answers to your questions or solutions to your problems. Begin by noticing a misplaced object, a surprising find, an unexpected emotion or a person that has particular meaning or relevance to your mission. Prepare for your creative session by asking the questions like: What am I already good at? What kind of business do I want to run? This may seem counter-intuitive, but if you begin your meditative journey with an open mind and some forethought, your subconscious will guide you through this uncharted voyage and continue to work on the questions you ask of it while you are on your safari. The concerted effort of conscious and unconscious thoughts will bring you surprising results. Voltaire pronounced, "No problem can withstand the assault of sustained thinking." Think productively, abundantly, and prosperously. Open your heart and mind to the greatness of your ideas.

You will find what you seek, but be patient. You may not find it the first time or even the next, but if you stay unencumbered by pretense and continue to explore in a variety of venues, you will learn to be creative, open-minded, and to look for details as well as the big picture. You just may find that elusive missing component of your plan or the psychological trap that's been restraining your imagination and hampering your progress. You will break free of it and the dogs of ambition will rule the night. Oh, never mind.

Number Two: The Mind Dump

Scoop up some sparking synapses and clean out your cranium. (alliteration brought to you courtesy of the grammar channel) The Mind Dump is not so much a brainstorming device as it is a brain clearing exercise. It's a gathering of collected data that you heap onto the work table in your idea room. Pick any wish you've kicked around either while on your brain safari or while coasting through life, something that you are drawn to and aren't sure why. Something that tugs at you. Then whip out the biggest piece of paper you can find and write the central thought down in the middle of the paper. Next, open your skull and dump everything you can think of that you can relate to the central theme onto that paper. No matter how remote the connection is; put it down. No plan, no organization. Just freely and joyfully dump it all out onto the paper. You can organize it later. This is not a time for outlines or other restrictions. This is a time to be free, unregulated by systems, or scary memories of your sixth grade composition teacher. (Mrs. Frankowski - who once punched me in the stomach for erasing a mistake I made in ink instead of rewriting the whole composition. I was eleven.) Let go and let it out. When you've exhausted all possible connections, put it aside and do something different from that activity. Go for a run, go for happy hour, call a friend, watch a movie or just sleep. Tomorrow you look at it. Tonight, let your subconscious work on what you've done. It will help you to streamline your ideas.

The next day, chunk your scattered thoughts into categories. Cobble together pieces of ideas and see if they transform into a better core idea. Is your primary thought something idealistic, like helping starving children, or a family business like a music store?

The creative connections will emerge as you record the data. For example; what are the loose connections to a music store? Let's see:

instruments	replacement parts	sheet music
lessons	musicians	bands
artists	repairs	style
education	sponsorships	music festivals
concerts	writing	custom instruments
theory	riffing	contests
competitions	jamming	open source access
expansion	another store	the bistro next door
sharing ideas	cultural changes	Algo mas?

Any item on that list can take you in a different direction, depending on where your heart is. Each connection opens another perspective. The Mind Dump is an attempt to break loose all the little ideas that you've had for years, but never acted on. Every time in your life that you've said, "Gee it would be neat if I could... or, If I owned this place I would change...Someday I'd like to..." Well all those nuggets are in there under stuff, behind other stuff, stuffed in stuff and enough is enough. Get it out there and take action.

The Mind Dump is not something you do over a cup of coffee. It takes some time. Good ideas need time to percolate. Your thoughts have been idle. Now you can plop this stew of ideas and memories onto your idea platform so you can sort through them to find what fits your 'why' in the most fulfilling and blissful way possible.

All memories are thoughts are connected in some way. On a molecular level, ideas and concepts are networks of neurons, so when you get a bright idea, it didn't just pop out of the ethers. It was wrought from smaller connections into one larger network which at some magical moment, forms a cohesive picture that captures your imagination. The big idea pops out in one "holy shit why didn't I think of that before" revelation. These creativity exercise help to find lost thoughts and new ways to enjoin them. Eventually your unified pieces of ideas will surge forward as one stroke of genius.

Number Three: Metathinking
The How of Thought

Metathinking is an awareness of how you are thinking and how you apply thought patterns to solve problems. It's not the act of thinking but how you think in a given situation.

So far your brain has been exposed to a little sunlight and a few seedlings are starting to pop out of the manure. Don't just accept them for what they appear. Look at your ideas from a variety of angles and see what's remarkable about them. Imagine you are proposing your ideas to a small group of influential people who could help you move your plan forward. Which idea can you easily describe?

Look at the big picture and work backwards (deductive reasoning). Look at specific pieces of a problem and work out from it (inductive reasoning). For example; if you want to open a business but can't decide which type you'd like to open, think about where you'd like to work, the social or work atmosphere that appeals to you. Think about businesses that you frequent. What draws you to them? Think about the type of lifestyle you require and the money needed to have it and then look for business ideas that fit the profile. The action of thinking is a progression of questions and answers.

Cognition is mental action; it's processes. Metacognition is the regulation of those processes. Meta is from the Greek for "after' or "beyond". It is a higher order of thinking that seems like an intellectual construct but is really just a learned method for applying the best type of thinking to generate ideas or solve problems.

Metacognition, or metathinking, is defined differently - the physical, mechanical or theoretical aspects - depending on the discipline in which the term is used. In the lexicon of neuroscience it is spoken of in terms of how the prefrontal cortex of our brain receives sensory input and deciphers it, then generates thoughts to define the input and categorize it. The brain scientists speak of executive management, which involves the monitoring and evaluating of your thought processes. Psychologists, by contrast, define it as self-evaluation. Military strategists think in terms of objectives and battle-driven adaptations. Architects use it to gain control over the struggle between form and function or in determining which craftsman is the best choice for handling a task.

Metacognition is also the application and/or testing of new strategies. It is a practice of actively controlling the manner in which we sort through objectives. Metacognition involves looking more closely at why we think the way we do and which types of circumstances or frames of mind drive that thinking. It's about choosing the best approach to a problem.

This mindset will help you focus but it will also put you in the habit of refocusing from new perspectives, which as we have discussed, leads to new insights. The metacognitive process is organic, meaning it naturally will evolve as you develop new approaches and try new styles and tactics. You will adapt your thinking as your platform expands.

Human beings have a great capacity for adaptive behavior. Metacognitive skills are cerebral cross-trainers; they help us run faster, jump higher and have more stamina in the learning and creative environments.

To develop these skills you must pause while you are working through a problem to think about your progress or the hindrances to the progress and then re-examine how you are thinking about the problem.

Are you on the right track? Are you centered on goals? Can you apply something you've already learned to your task?

What kinds of problems are you facing in your life design: funding, access, resources, family, logistics, health or support? Honest assessment is a big step toward higher order thinking. Don't try to fix symptoms without recognizing their underlying cause. "Architecture is the reaching out for the truth." – Louis Kahn

Collectively, this book is a metacognitive process. Metacognition is thinking in a more organized way. It's solution-directed thinking. When you finally arrive at a solution, make time to review the thought processes that helped you or enabled breakthroughs, so you can apply them to your next set of problems.

Thinking is physically draining. According to Richard Restak, your brain is a glutton for energy. Although your brain is only 2% of your total body weight, it receives 15% of the cardiac output, 20% of the total body oxygen you consume, and a whopping 25% of total body glucose used. Since we will use so much of our energy stores in the cognitive process, it will serve you better to examine the way you think so you can do it more efficiently and productively.

Make time to wonder about how small changes will have an impact on your overall design. When I was writing this book, I always thought about the following chapter and how the one I was writing would fit into the next. Like a stone mason, carving one stone helps to define the shape of the one that follows. I tried to think from the perspective of a designer. How will this piece effect the next wave of ideas? What will be the thought or phrase that links one element to another? Eero Saarinen put it cohesively, "Always consider a thing by considering it in its next larger context – a chair in a room, a room in a house, a house in an environment, an environment in a city plan."

Even though I had no formal training, I imagined, "If I was an architect; what would be my next move? What seems to flow naturally from where I am?" Each element must complement, support, build upon, inspire transition, elevate, enliven, strengthen, and articulate the evolving plan. It works the way a foundation to a home supports the frame, which complements the design features that transition to the outdoor space and reflect the surrounding environment.

Metathinking is the aide-de-camp of general focus. It keeps you from permitting distractions that may pull you off your course of successful thinking. Distractions are predominantly caused by a lack of discipline. How will you deal with them and stay on goal? Are you disciplined? What is your study or learning environment like? Is the television on? Don't tell me it helps you think. That's preposterous. It helps you avoid thinking.

Is your chair comfortable?
Are you sufficiently nourished and rested?
Will you have positive thought patterns?
Will your patterns be productive?
Are you mindful of the details as well as the big picture?
Do you think in terms of action/impact/goals?

Challenge yourself to explore different modalities of thought. Thomas Edison never picked anything up without thinking about how he could improve it.

Metacognition helps you to gain control over your thinking processes. You must plot out the type and duration of thinking that will be needed to accomplish a given task. It helps in all aspects of learning and planning. Studies show students with high metacognitive skills work more efficiently. They are self-directed and naturally remain focused. They draw on lessons learned from other learning tasks and apply them to the job at hand. It sounds tricky at first but by making attempts to recognize how you are thinking as you form each level, you will eventually become a natural meta-thinker.

Think about designing and building a bird house. Seems simple enough. But what if your design was an entry into a competition for design school or help for an endangered species? How would this change your approach? Would you include windows, vents, roofing & siding? Would you need to consider size, color, protection from predators, the potential for breeding? Context changes your thinking.

The physicist, Dr. Debbie Berebichez, says she always wears her physicist glasses. She is always looking at the world through the lens of science. Try changing the way you view your world. Visit a design gallery or read a book that is different from your usual fair, unroll a cigar, take a toy apart, design an end table, read naval strategy, identify every tree on your block and note what's different about each one. Walk a route that you would normally drive. Visualize the way back before you return.

Visualize it from overhead or under ground. Look up at the architecture of your city. Notice how one building fits with those around it and how together they form the cityscape. Explore a new city and wonder what is involved in the running of that city: planning, sewer systems, gas lines, garbage removal, drinking water, historical preservation, fire service and code enforcement. Note how the systems interact or depend upon one another. Ruminating will help you assemble your life plan cohesively. You'll feed details to the big picture.

Number Four - The Coffee Klatsch
or for you German students - Der Kaffeeklatsch

Stephen Johnson, best-selling author of "Where Good Ideas Come From," has conducted extensive research into innovation and the stuff of good ideas. He believes that the common image of a scientist who has a eureka moment comes from movies and not reality. Thoughts and the millions of neurons that link together to make them are, physiologically speaking, networks, so they thrive in socially interactive spaces.

The best ideas are the soufflés of your brain; they need time to rise. There is a tipping point of inspiration that presents itself as a violà moment, but good ideas really come about because of time and place. They need time to percolate and an environment that is conducive to sharing them. Steven Johnson discusses the first coffee and tea houses of England in the 17th century in his book and argues that it was these places where like minded writers, scientists, philosophers and other scholars came together and exposed their thoughts and inspirations to criticism, counter and supporting arguments, and general banter, that led to the significant cultural movement in western history know as The Enlightenment, the Age of Reason.

Good ideas flourish when they are exposed to the light of day. There have been too many times when I have written a brilliant passage after midnight, only to discover at ten the next morning that what I wrote was crap. Some of us manic-depressive, alcoholic writers find we work more fluidly in the later hours (fluid being the key word), and although self-absorbed torment fuels great novels, in your quest for an extraordinary life you must enlist others for help, a kind of thought intervention.

You need your friends for grounding. You can get caught up in the moment of your revelation, imagining only the best possible outcome for implementing your cool idea. "When I sell this thing to Google, I'll be worth millions." But what separates us from the farm animals is our capacity for delusion. Ideas need a forum to be observed. They need a place to linger in the collective energy of your mentors and friends.

Philip Frelon explains that innovation happens in an organic way, "when ideas are put on the table and discussed. And that the question remains suspended in the air for a while before a solution settles to the ground, and that can only happen in the kind of environment that encourages communication and introspection at all levels."

By hearing your thoughts aloud, bouncing them off your support team or asking for input from experienced people, your ugly ideas will emerge as the swans you envisioned.

Your thoughts need to be kicked around, prodded, expanded and filtered through a process that is best undertaken around the kitchen table over a steaming pot of fair-trade coffee and almond biscottis. Challenge yourself. Up your own stakes. Raise the standard you set for yourself. Think about joining or forming a mastermind group, but leave your ego home. As Randy Gage says, "If you're the smartest person in your group, get another group."

What you and I really need is balance. Some of us who are more introverted will do really well with the Brain Safari, while those more extroverted will like the coffee house idea. Ideally, you need solitude for deep thought, but your ideas need interaction to develop.

7 Quick Strategies for Generating Ideas

1 - **Let your subconscious work for you**. Use the most powerful tool in your war chest. I'm sure you've had the experience of not being able to recall an actor's name during a conversation and then three hours later in the shower you remember - Wilford Brimley. It's happened to me and similar things have happened to all of us, which is proof enough of the parallel functioning of our subconscious minds.

Your brain is a potent organ. But you have to believe in it and allow it to function. Your brain has the ability to uptake vast amounts of information, all in some way linked to stuff you already know. You can trust your brain to travel back through these connections to help your mind find solutions.

Write down what's troubling you just before you go to sleep; you don't have to tuck it under your pillow. While you sleep your brain consolidates ideas and flushes out the twitter - no offense. Many of Ana

Manzo's designs are initially propagated by dreams. She allows herself to be informed by them, trusting enough in herself to allow them space to breathe in her studio. Lest you think this is light-hearted musings, there is mounting scientific discussion about dreams as an emergence of unresolved issues, sifted external stimuli and productive subconscious activity. In his best-selling book, "Blink", professor Malcolm Gladwell describes rapid cognition, demonstrating how what happens on the subconscious level is thinking; but it's thinking that happens so rapidly it evades conscious observation, remaining locked in the subconscious and becoming manifest through emotions and dreams. Ana is an open person, both professionally and spiritually. This openness invites the observations in the ethers to occupy her. So her dreams are a way of getting in touch with all perceptions of creative energy, and that is ultimately what she draws on for inspiration. "Thanks to them that today I am the woman I am...through my dreams, I hope you can understand a little of what I have come to discover..."

2 - **Quotes and Quips**. The great thing about quotations is the big wad of wisdom that's packed into a short statement. Read from a broad spectrum of quotes, including sports, business, art, science, humor, innovation, medicine and personal dynamics. Develop the habit of relating what they say to your personal situation. Reading quotes about architecture started an entire second career for me.

3 - **Read Wikipedia with random abandon**. Get wild-eyed about it, like a mad wikipediac. Recklessly and enthusiastically click on the blue link-letters (Art was ahead of his time) and travel thru open-source cyberspace. Wikipedia literally opens up your PC to the knowledge of the world. Read it until your brain hurts. Eventually you will land on something fascinating enough to jolt your creative impulses.

4 - **Why Can't I?** Pranav Mistry is a PhD student at MIT. He is the inventor of SixthSense, a wearable device that enables interactions between the real world and the world of data. He also invented a digital pen that draws in 3D, an awesome tool for architects. The list of his mind-blowing inventions is quite long, and all preceded by Pranav asking, "Why not? Why can't I do this? Why can't my gestures from the physical

world be displayed in the digital world?" By asking questions this way he challenges the world to prove him wrong and so far, he hasn't lost.

Watch this TED talk, "The Thrilling Potential of Sixth Sense Technology." Count how many times he says that his ideas came from asking himself, "Why can't I?" This type of question is personally challenging, which stimulates brain activity.

Some have said that this kind of question affirms a negative, that it sets your brain up to tell you precisely why you cannot. But if you look at the question in the context of a personal challenge; it sends a different message, one that prods you to perform. It is an attitude that says. "Don't tell me I can't - I will show you otherwise."

5 - **Lateral Pollination** - You can stimulate creativity by pushing yourself to think about overlapping disciplines. It's a cross application of ideas. In my Catholic grammar school we had a homeroom, which we left to file (quietly) down the hall to arithmetic class, which we then left to go to history and so on it went. We were left to our own devices to figure out how it all worked together, how art influenced history or how history influenced language. Art class was pretty much macaroni sculptures and gold spray paint. Creative thinking was not encouraged.

Ask crazy questions. How would a vegetable farmer solve the teen pregnancy problem? How would a mathematician describe a pathogen? How can we understand world religions by studying trade routes? By turning to seemingly disparate disciplines for answers you can find innovative applications for your ideas.

6 - **Comedy** - Inventive performers like Eddie Izzard are funny because they make uncommon connections. Psychologist and psychometrician, Robert Sternberg, says "Synthetic ability is what we typically think of as creativity. It is the ability to generate novel and interesting ideas. Often the person we call creative is a particularly good synthetic thinker who makes connections between things that other people do not recognize spontaneously." CGI allows film makers to connect traditional roles to unusual personality types, so we end up falling in love with the big-hearted swamp creatures and sword-fighting gatos.

One of the fun aspects of Twitter is reading how people pack so much cleverness into 140 characters. It's a creative challenge.

Take time to examine the incongruous connections comedians

make. It's a great way to observe creative minds at work. So watch some stand-up and if you get accused of loafing you can honestly say you're conducting research.

7 - **Do Nothing**. "Everybody's doing something. We'll do nothing!" - George Castanza.

By doing nothing I mean real leisure. Put the project aside and go play with the kids, take your spouse to a movie or get a hot rock massage. Sometimes we get so caught up in trying to force ideas, we end up with cerebral performance anxiety. There is no blue pill for this. Just get away, relax, reach out to someone important that you've been neglecting. Tell your parents you're proud of them. Borrow 1700 dollars and go to a Yankee game with your only child. Time away from the mission will rejuvenate you. Enthusiasm is uplifting and your brain works much more effectively when it is relieved of stress.

These seven strategies are meant to enhance your insight ability, described by Robert Sternberg in his <u>Triarchic Theory of Intelligence</u>. It's simply putting problems in different contexts to develop novel solutions. Architecture is appreciated in part because of perspective. It's how architects solve problems, how they work with the landscape, how they incorporate their designs with the dynamics of the city and how they determine the manner in which we move through the space.

But don't rest on one solution. Often creative people are grinders. They stick with problems longer and try new angles of attack until they find a workable connection. What may seem like a good idea is really the first piece of a better idea. Give it time. Play with it. Nurture it.

Ideas vs. Ideation

Ideas are passive, easy to conceive. But ideation is active. Ideation is the mechanics of ideas, their construction and procedures. Ideation is not thought; it is the testing of thoughts. Architects excel at this skill, which is the exploration of the possibilities of an idea and the conceivable outcomes of its application, based upon whacking it with assorted stimuli. Testing ideas is how the pros innovate, from architects, to engineers, to scientists and finally, to you. We never lose the thrill of discovering something new; what we lose is our zest for finding it. When we work on developing ideas that interest us, that touch us emotionally, that are goal oriented; they pull us into a feeling of, "Yes, yes, this is it. This is fun. This is an exciting step forward." To do this we must believe in and trust, our natural eagerness for adventure and tap into our education and experiences. It's fun, dammit. In fact it can be downright exhilarating. When we are in a state of exhilarated innovation, powered by our burn to succeed, ideation can flow unconstrained by anchors or convention. It is a pure state of creativity. It is the state described in "Flow" by Mihaly Csikczentmihalyi. In this state you can invent or reinvent anything, even yourself.

A Last Thought on Creativity

There is no need to judge your creative expertise, but there is a need to develop the habits of innovation, such as conceptual thinking, presenting those concepts in schematics or drawings, sharing ideas, and changing perspective. This book is here to help get the juices flowing. It won't help you design the world's most inspiring art gallery, but it may help you get back into school so you can study design. It won't make you Richard Branson, but it will help you get out of a drab job and form a business service company. You have majesty inside you, but you must first figure out what you want and what needs improvement.

Level One is about getting a sense of what it means to think imaginatively but with an eye toward sustainability, goals and process. We can't paint like Van Gogh or write like Cormac McCarthy; these men are supernovas in their field. But that shouldn't stop you from trying to be better at whatever ignites your passions. If I could write like McCarthy I would, but I can't... so I can only look under my pillow and see if the tough-shit fairy left me anything.

You can learn to behave creatively - to think about expanding your context, trusting intuition, trying variety, changing orientation and the hierarchy of thoughts.

You will have ideas. Post them on the wall. Story-board your ideas like a film plot or magazine layout. Open the space of your ideas from your mind to your work environment. This is the kind of work you should be having fun with even though you might agonize over it. It's for a good purpose. This is the start of better version of you. You will become increasingly proud of your abilities as you progress through seven levels. By the time you are finished you will be eager to pass along what you have learned and use your skills to tackle another project. You'll want to live to be a hundred and seven, brimming with ideas and the confidence to work on them.

In phase two the architects and their clients decide on a final design and then begin the work of planning to build it. In Level Two you will make a final decision about the direction of your life design, but not before you explore all options that present themselves in Level One.

Steven Holl says, "Architecture is an organic link between concept and form. The idea drives the design." So now that you have an idea, let's give it substance.

Level Two
Precision has Purpose

"Architecture arouses sentiments in man. The architect's task, therefore, is to make those sentiments more precise." – Adolf Loos

L evel Two is about making a decision and giving your idea substance. Now that you've had a little fun exploring your creative side, it's time to get serious and choose a life design from the three or four best choices you've posted on the wall in your work space. (You did that, right?) It's time to move from ideas to precise action. The nexus between ideas and action is a decision. It's a decision to let loose the anchors of fear, doubt and excuses. It's a decision to pick one path and stick to it through the completion of your journey, impervious to the slings and arrows of outrageous envy.

So you've had a few failures in life or gotten lousy advice (that you followed) and maybe the forces that shaped your childhood are still strong. The scars are deep and the emotional current runs thick with angst. Oh well, so what? What's a little anxiety? Humans have survived tornados, plagues, locusts and flaming monkeys; I think you can get through another blue day. Toughen up. When you make a decision to no longer allow the past to determine your future, you kick open the tall double doors to a new and hopeful horizon. Funny thing about horizons, each time you reach one another appears just ahead.

Let's decide together. What is your mission? What's stopping you from acting now? All of us have had ideas that we never saw materialize.

Why? Action. What's the difference between you and the guy on that TV show explaining how he made his millions? Action. "What have they got that I haven't got? Courage." In designing your life you must have the courage to make the decision. This decision will be the cornerstone of your mission.

In Level Two you decide upon the one thing that will complete your life in a fulfilling way. It doesn't mean you're not already a great parent or friend, but this is the one thing you will be better at than anything else, the feature of you that people think of when they hear your name. You can be a jack of all trades but there are only so many DaVincis, so many Renaissance men. Michael Jordan can play baseball and golf but not the way he played basketball. Brian Leetch was a great baseball player yet he became a hockey Hall of Fame legend playing defense for the New York Rangers.

The concept of this level is to focus your vague ideas in a drawing, outline or model and make a final determination of what your project will be. Giving your ideas a sort of physicality will help you make an informed choice. The always thoughtful Brad Cloepfil stated, "I think architects and architecture is best at clarifying things. I think there's sort of many camps of architecture obviously, in that way. Architects have always tried to be propositional, to be proposers of new ideas, but I actually think that they're best at condensing and filtering and compacting and concentrating ideas."

In architecture the two basic elements of design are aesthetics and utility - how it will look and how it will work. I realize that's like describing a Mozart piano concerto as being made up of black keys and white keys, but it's a start. In your life design, the two basic elements are prosperity and fulfillment. How will the time devoted to this project bring prosperity to my life and those I care about? How will this project fulfill me emotionally, intellectually and spiritually? Will this bold idea broaden my base of operations for further exploration? Will it bring abundance to my life? What legacy or lessons will I pass on? Bill Pedersen said, "Architecture is a very visible and permanent record of the hopes and aspirations of the culture. Those buildings that we leave behind are an obvious example of what our intentions were as a civilization."

Will your design stretch you? Will it test you? Will it be long-lasting, desirable or teachable? Will it help you form a heritage of goal seekers, even if only for your immediate family?

Try something that runs counter to your primary inclinations. Move into your discomfort zone, the place where you feel self-doubt. Each time you produce in your discomfort zone, you expand your existing arena of skills. You become comfortable in a larger zone of operations. When you have completed the modeling phase of this level, you will have a clear-minded purpose without which you cannot advance. You will have a cornerstone to build upon.

In construction, the cornerstone sets the direction of the exterior courses. The other lines are oriented from it.

According to an entry in Wikimedia (08/2011), "The cornerstone (or foundation stone) concept is derived from the first stone set in the construction of masonry foundation, important, since all other stones will be set in reference to this stone, thus determining the position of the entire structure." So your second level sets the perspective of your project. Everything you build from this point will be anchored by and set in reference to this decision.

"Over time a cornerstone became a ceremonial masonry stone, or replica, set in a prominent location on the outside of a building, with an inscription on the stone indicating the construction dates of the building and the names of the architect, builder and other significant individuals. The rite of laying a cornerstone is an important cultural component of eastern architecture metaphorically, and sacred architecture, generally."

As you progress through your process, you will always refer back to this stone, this decision, the primary goal. Therefore, you must have compelling reasons why you choose a particular direction. It represents the 'why' of your mission.

During this second phase, the architects undertake feasibility studies to dissect the issues that may hinder the project. They determine a game plan for dealing with site analysis, soil, water and wind testing. They consider power supplies; fossil fuels or green sources. Time lines are established. And of course, questions are asked. How will the design strategy stress the budget? Is the plan feasible given the fiscal and time constraints? Are existing structures in good repair; are they structurally sound? What must be torn down or what can be saved/altered? Is this a flood plain or are there concerns about earthquakes? This is a kind of "if-then" thinking that helps to settle on a firm verdict.

This is also when a common vocabulary for the venture is created.

This ensures that team members will understand one another when discussing various aspects of the project, limiting misinterpretations of assignments. When planning your levels, consistent vocabulary or terminology will help you internalize your project. You will avoid ambiguity which may lead to digressions or confusion at plan intervals.

After this exacting process the detailed plans are drawn up or configured with a computer-aided design program. These are the blueprints the builders use for the actual construction.

> A side note – Blueprints are actually a term of art for the reproduction of the technical drawing. They were once printed on linen, but eventually advanced to be printed on Mylar, with that familiar Prussian blue color we recognize. The term 'blueprint' has evolved to mean the detailed plans for architecture, engineering etc. I use it in this book to refer to any batch of detailed plans, your power-packed action plans.

The decision you render in Level Two must clear and easy to articulate. It is the core idea. In architecture, this is known as the parti, (par-TEE), or the informing concept of the building. It is the story of your design. The parti for Frank Lloyd Wright's <u>Falling Water</u> is a home that is congruent with nature.

In order to define your core concept you must sift through the creative exercises of Level One and find your golden nugget. During this process you discard ideas that aren't appealing. You latch on to the most exhilarating idea, and target your most compelling future vision. Clarity of purpose is energizing. Precision is the grail you seek in Level Two. It is a singular, life-altering, transformational decision. Whether you seek restoration or reincarnation, the final product requires transformation. It requires a change of thinking, a change of desire, a change from wishes to action and a change of standpoint. You must decide not merely to move with purpose, but to move on purpose. Like we said when we were kids, "He did it on purpose." You must be clear and purposeful from this point forward.

When you work on exercises like the retail space, you begin to appreciate the value of channeling ideas. Architects don't create entire skylines, but they may start one, or enhance another. They are sometimes city planners but they are generally planners with a specific purpose. So often, our own dreamscapes are abstract. We must create a clear denotation in Level Two. On the first level you explored your creative side. Now you must settle on a schema. You must reflect upon what happened during your exercises. What was the most fun for you? What startled you? What discoveries did you make about yourself? What struck a nerve, excited you or rekindled a fire? Did you finally accept what you've known you were good at all along?

Focus

The second step is all about getting specific. From this level you will establish a clear path toward your design. In the world of architecture, the second phase is the making of a sketch or model of the project, a physical representation of ideas for review by clients, benefactors or the professors. It gives their ideas an organic composition. This is critical to bringing ideas to life, to making lasting impressions and creating the plans of success. Your ideas are a little scattered right now because it was important that your creative realm had no walls. Similarly, technological innovation flourishes in part because of the open architecture of the internet. Ideas are claustrophobic. Let them breath. However, once you've decided on a course of action, you should develop a drawing, a pointed summary or a model of your vision.

You may want to begin with a rough outline. Include key phrases in the text that resonate with you. My sketch of the seven levels included core ideas such as aspiration, human endeavor, process, the lure of triumph, why architecture matters, the four warrior concept and correlations/ connections to the built world.

Tony Robbins says, "Clarity is power." We say, "Precision has purpose." Say it any way you wish, as long as you understand that vagaries cannot be accomplished. Wimpy goals are easily distracted. Fractured ideas are indefinable and hence, impossible to plan around. In his book, "101 Things I Learned in Architecture School", Matthew Frederick states, "The more specific an idea is, the greater its appeal is likely to be. Being non-specific in an effort to appeal to everyone usually results in reaching no one. But drawing upon a specific observation, poignant statement, ironic point, witty reflection, intellectual connection, political argument, or idiosyncratic belief in a creative work can help you create environments others will identify with in their own way."

I could have expressed my ideas about personal development in generic terms, but by specifically relating them to the architectural process, I allow you to make any connection to the built world that you can relate to. Everyone has some important event in their life that they can connect to a built place. This concept, though specific, is not limited. It still permits personal architectural associations to move you. Brad Cloepfil said, "Innovation is less of a concern to me than specificity. I think each project, each problem, each city, each context offers its own set of solutions and its own kind of material possibilities. Each city has its own character. Each climate has its own nature. So I think the more specific we can make the buildings, the more resonant they are, the more they communicate the possibilities of architecture in that particular place and particular culture. So it's not a drive to make new things; it's a drive to make excruciatingly specific things."

Now that you understand how to generate ideas, the next challenge lies in making them actionable. The difference between ideas that don't advance and ideas that come to pass is in the clarity of your purpose. You cannot take action without clarity of purpose. Fuzzy ideas bring ambiguous results, or no results at all.

Find a way in one coherent, statement to express your purpose and to persuade your support team to stick with you. "My purpose for writing The Seventh Level is to become the best person in the world to speak about the application of the architectural process to human endeavor." That is it in one sentence. It might be a little ballsy but as William Zinsser stated in On Writing Well, "Sell yourself, and your subject will exert its own appeal. Believe in your own identity and your own opinions. Proceed with confidence, generating it, if necessary, by pure willpower. Writing is an act of ego and you might as well admit it. Use its energy to keep yourself going." So maybe it takes a splash of ego to think anyone cares what I have to say, but I'm saying it anyway.

Think lean. Pare your mission down to its most fundamental, the black and white keys. Don't be shy about cutting. Some ideas seem great at first, but when fleshed out, lose their pizzazz. Don't be attached to an idea that may have been moderately useful before. As R. Buckminster Fuller pointed out, "I am enthusiastic over humanity's extraordinary and sometimes very timely ingenuity. If you are in a shipwreck and all the boats are gone, a piano top buoyant enough to keep you afloat that comes along makes a fortuitous life preserver. But this is not to say that the best way to design a life preserver is in the form of a piano top. I think that we are clinging to a great many piano tops in accepting yesterday's fortuitous contrivings as constituting the only means for solving a given problem." Throwing out some of your original ideas may actually be liberating. They were only frustrating you anyway.

The Drawing

Architects need a medium to express their ideas. Drawings filled that need until computer-aided design (CAD) came into practice. But drawings are still widely used by designers to convey ideas, and to help develop those ideas into a coherent visual statement. Their sketches are used to resolve practical issues or to try new ideas and discard old ones, long before the final plans are set and money is spent. During the idea/sketch phase our options are limitless, but once we commit to a plan, they become narrowed, limited to moving the plan forward, rather than continually shifting direction. The sketches are tools for thought. In drawing them, you must develop the big ideas first. Matthew Frederick relates this concept as drawing hierarchically. "When drawing in any medium, never work at 100% level of detail from one end of the sheet to the other, blank end of the sheet. Instead, start with the most general elements of the composition and work gradually toward the more specific aspects of it."

There are many types of drawing in the business of architecture and construction: preliminary drawings of concepts, working drawings, shop and mechanical drawing, to list a handful, but they all serve a central purpose, which is to convey ideas.

The cognitive bias known as the picture superiority effect means humans are more likely to remember a concept experientially, one that incorporates verbal and imagery memory systems, when the concept is presented with more than mere words. Real images lead to real plans. "Architecture is a manifold of space, light and material in time." - Steven Holl.

The issues of concern to the architect are expressed in drawings. "Practical concerns include space allocated for different activities, how people enter and move around the building, daylight and artificial lighting, acoustics, traffic noise, legal matters and building codes, and many other issues. While both aspects (aesthetic & practical) are partly a matter of customary practice, every site is different. Many architects actively seek innovation, thereby increasing the number of problems to be resolved." - Wikipedia - "Architectural Drawing" (November 03, 2011).

Having trouble getting started? "Draw the box it came in." Matthew Frederick teaches that building design can have rectilinear aspects, that is, they are drawn by straight lines. But what if you are designing cars or furniture? If you are unsure where to begin, then borrow this concept from architecture. Draw the box your project comes in. Let's say you want to open a small, storefront business. What <u>box</u> or location will it come in? How will you approach your store? Will it be in a mall, on a street corner, in a strip mall, a hotel lobby or will it be free-standing? These are the boxes that stores come in, so it may help to begin there and work toward your own business.

Through the sketching/modeling phase you will begin to solve the problems that have hampered your prior success. In the words of Ellen Yi-Luen Do, "The act of drawing is a form of design reasoning." She believes that nearly all problems are solved though sketches. Japanese architect Tadao Ando has said, "My hand is the extension of the thinking process."

Models

Models create perspective. In this digital age we see everything on little screens. The internet has opened the world to us but our perspective of these new places is flat. We don't sense or smell them. We don't feel the energy or history. You can look at images of the Roman Coliseum but to be there, to feel the stone, to stand in it, to know the magnitude of death and triumph of that place, can give you chills. Without a physical presence your ideas are flat.

Ideally, when you have a completed drawing, you should construct a model of your idea, or what your idea represents, to present it with a sense of animation. Think in dynamic terms, action words that energize and entertain. The three-dimensional aspect draws you into the piece. The model highlights scale and proportion, so you can begin to really feel the emerging life force.

If you cannot make a physical model then create a diagram of your plan, using general terms to label major aspects. Working through this phase helps to develop the logic of your design. It may also uncover design flaws for you to fix. In architecture, a finished product may go through unanticipated and expensive changes along the way. This is why it is obviously critical to complete the design and blueprints before the actual construction work starts. Working this way is efficient and efficiency should be part of your work paradigm. Time is valuable, in the architectural world and in your own.

We rarely place a value on our time outside of our regular work environment. We will make an irrational decision to waste half a day driving across town to save 20 bucks. We don't calculate the monetary value of the time we lose in chasing the cash. Make the time to determine what your time is worth and what it will be worth when you have finished your schooling or training. Think of your time in terms of money. Sit down with a pencil and calculate the financial loss brought on by your inefficiency and wasteful habits.

When I was a teenager I painted houses with a guy named Tommy Kosakowski. He was a tough kid from Bayonne, NJ who taught me about efficiency. He once watched me rolling paint on a wall and noticed I was using too little paint, trying to force it out of the roller, which takes more time and is more physically demanding. "Joe, paints cheap - labor's expensive." I learned that a proper application of the material and the correct use of my tools helped to smooth the work flow and save time, which I repeat, is expensive. In your life design there will be tools at your disposal that will make your work easier, professional and efficient. You must learn to find the right tools and use them for optimal performance. If you don't know, ask your mentors.

Context

How does my idea fit into the whole context of my life? Will it be disruptive to my current life and is that necessarily a bad thing?

During the second phase of architecture, the other experts are brought in. To complete your second level you must determine who your mentors and partners should be, who you may require financial support from, who can provide guidance and leadership, and who might provide the emotional support during your dark days. This will determine your team so you can incorporate them into the detailed plans when the time comes.

Architects draw site plans to see the structure in context with the surrounding city center or landscape. Does the footprint fit the site? What do the engineers, city planners, surveyors and landscapers think?

By placing the building idea in its proper context, the architect may see potential problems. By putting your own ideas in context, you can see your plan from the perspective of those it will impact. That change in perspective will provide more insight to the best way to proceed.

Alan Kay said, "Perspective is worth 80 IQ points." That's not a bad advantage. Your sketch, when presented to your support team, will elicit questions, potential hazards and hopefully, a few atta-boys. You may discover surprise opportunities.

Practical Retail Exercise

For this exercise, assume you are leaning you toward starting a small business. Assume you like to travel and you enjoy local artistry. You have an eye for design; you're detail oriented and good with people. You think you might open a small specialty import business, a scaled-down version of the famous "Pier One Imports." Let's call it Seven Levels of One World.

This exercise will teach you to think contextually. The idea at this stage is to ask overarching questions to help decide what your concept will be. You are learning to sketch and model here. The next level of detail will be defined in the planning phase of Level Three.

What size is your operation? Do you see mom & pop or room for expansion? Will you buy goods from around the world or focus on a particular region such as southeast Asia? Will your imports be tilted toward home furnishings, home decor, personal accessories or a combination? Will you carry original art? What is your client base or to whom do you want to sell (working/middle class, wealthy)?

Draw your store from the view of the customer. What is it about the exterior that entices them to walk in? What do they see when they enter? Is there a theme or style? What's your "I gotta have that" item?

Create the interior layout. Include a rough floor plan and displays. Draw it, then build a cardboard model of it. Don't worry if it's imperfect; just do it. Use your fifth grader's construction paper and paste. Let her help.

Now draw your store from the perspective of the owner. Think about positioning, flow, inventory control, storage, counter space, employees and point-of-sale purchases, those little impulse items we're all guilty of buying at the register. Think about names, themes or the personality of the place. Do you have large and small items for sale? How will you display both?

These answers will form the basic elements of your business. They will identify the parti of your enterprise. (Don't forget to have fun.)

There is still much work to be done, questions to be answered and theories to be tested. Edmund Bacon said, "It's in the doing that the idea comes." Doug Patt, who is a master at edifying us about architecture with his internet videos, says that drawing is "the best way" to find solutions to problems. This book, by its existence, represents the veracity of the seven level system. As I write it, I recognize that I am not an expert in this field. But my research, along with my discussions with my mentors in developing the theories, and its public and practical applications, are a strong beginning toward that expertise. I will learn from mistakes and improve my content; that's what "the doing" does.

The more problems architects solve, the more innovative they can become. It's like the learning continuum - the more you learn, the more you can learn. The deeper and wider your foundation - the higher and wider the building. The stronger the core structure - the more peripheral elements it can support. Over many years of working through this philosophy, architects exceed their own potential and so can you. The culmination of small achievements will bring prosperity to your life, if you are open to it. But to be open to prosperity you must first purge the negativity to make room for it. Having done that, you begin to feel fulfilled. You will enjoy the abundance you seek.

Have you named your project? Now would be a good time. Matthew Frederick says when you name your project it helps "explain to yourself what you have created." I don't agree with that statement specifically because you should definitely be able to explain your own project to yourself, but I agree that naming your project can give it personality. It makes it yours and helps with a sense of ownership. Naming your project helps to make it a process. By calling this book The Seventh Level I had to create the process of building one level upon the other. I had to write a process for each level and a link to connect them, otherwise this book would be really short. It would be impractical as a tool.

Authors name their projects. They use working titles for the work in progress. They often change as the characters develop and the story emerges, but giving the manuscript a title has a way of priming the pump.

Now your pumping. You've learned to think imaginatively, decided on your mission and given it a name. It's now time to configure the blueprints. It's time to carefully and thoroughly write your extraordinary plan.

Level Three
The Big Hairy Plans

"Make not little plans; they have no magic to stir men's blood and probably themselves will not be realized. Make big plans; aim high in hope and work, remembering that a noble, logical diagram once recorded will never die, but long after we are gone will a living thing, asserting itself with ever-growing insistency." - Daniel H. Burnham

Congratulations! You've decided on something. Now let's plan your mission precisely and thoroughly. Your level of belief in your idea will determine the quality of action you take and the ferocity with which you will execute it. The intensity of your actions will determine your results. When you achieve those results, you will bolster your belief in your abilities. But you can't just do a Haka and charge on to the rugby field of life; you need a plan. You need a strategy.

The general design phase is set and now you begin drilling down to the sometimes mundane but always necessary details. Your plan begins as a conceptual framework to support your ideas and help them connect in a logical sequence, so don't completely turn off your right brain yet; just start leaning a little heavier on the left. Identify your universe, then chunk by chunk, break your plan down to the smallest detail.

You won't read but a few quotations from architects about blueprints and planning because there really is nothing profound about it. Although there are many facets and potential pitfalls to consider, a plan is simply the order in which things must be done. When you built Levels One and

Two you were dreaming, aspiring, imagining, hoping and challenging your paradigms. On Level Four you will make a dramatic personal change. These are emotionally charged concepts that lend themselves to eloquent thoughts. But the planning - squished between aspiration and rejuvenation - is a patient plotting out of the programmatic elements. It's a mapping of the logical sequence of actions, strung together in the most effective way possible to reach your goal. Like a business plan, it represents you. You are the business your plan represents. Even if your mission is not a traditional business-specific idea but rather tilted toward the birthing of a new self, then you can still fashion your plan in a business model, which would include: core strategies, timing, financing, competition, your products, services and the value that you can add to the lives of your customers. Treat yourself like a business and take the planning seriously. You wouldn't just hang a sign and hope for the best; you would conduct research, secure advice and have a solid strategy in place. The business plan concept is just that, a concept, like many more available to you and limited only by the impediments you put in the way of your imagination.

As you make your plans; remember these words of Antoine de Saint-Exupéry, "Quand tu veux construire un bateau, ne commence pas par rassembler du bois, couper des planches et distribuer du travail, mais reveille au sein des hommes le desir de la mer grande et large." Wait, hang on; that's a note for my maid. Here it is - "If you want to build a ship, don't drum up people together to collect wood and don't assign them tasks and work, but rather teach them to long for the endless immensity of the sea." Set your soul ablaze. Think magnificent thoughts first, then work the plans. Remember your reasons why you are doing this. As Brendon Burchard says, "It's not a hobby." Take this seriously and plan with fervor. What could be more important than the blueprint of your life?

Old blueprints are art because of the visionary who created them, not just because the lines are pretty. Some architectural drawings are considered art and I would agree if we were discussing presentation drawings or concepts pieces, but to my mind they are artistic because they represent the possibility of living architecture, the imagining of a real place. The detailed blueprints of your personal plan are merely renditions of the materials, sequences, actions and time frames, carefully wrought - nothing astonishing. It is the ideal behind the plans that is important. For example, the opening of a new Farallon Islands Marine

Sanctuary in San Francisco, California might be hailed as a glorious event, but someone has to build it first. Someone has to lay out precisely how many yards of concrete will be poured, how many tons of steel or stone must be ordered, what must be specially made, what must be crafted by an artisan, which type of wood will be used for the built-in cabinets in the infirmary. The blueprints may be huge, but they are not romantic.

A plan should be a realistic depiction of your ladder of expectations. It should consist, much as your ladder, of a series of steps, each with a specific task designed to lead you to your goal. Be conscientious in the planning phase because it is the route you must follow through until your mission is complete. Once you finish the plan, you should not deviate from it without heartfelt consideration, re-planning, and a little anguish. Would you take a sudden lateral step while climbing a ladder? Not without painful consequences.

Although even a brilliantly conceived plan will not guarantee success, no plan will almost certainly guarantee failure. It's not that plans cannot change. In fact, they will be developed, refined and improved. A good designer knows when to let go of something that isn't working and try a fresh solution.

Some of the ideas you modeled for Level Two, may turn out to be impractical as you uncover the next level of detail. Don't try to force them. Let it flow. My original concept for this book was to spotlight one architect for each of the seven levels, one who embodied the spirit of the particular chapter or represented the individual ideals. So, for example, I might discuss Paul Williams in Level Four because that chapter is about breaking ground for your foundation and he was a ground-breaker as a black architect in Los Angeles in the 30's and 40's.

But as I began to write I realized I was limiting my readers to only one architect's opinions about each phase of the design process. With so many brilliant architects in the world, this narrow view short-changed my audience. I was cutting out wisdom and insight that would make the learning experience richer by limiting each chapter to one emblematic viewpoint. While conducting my research I collected piles of quotes and stories about architects that applied across the spectrum of building philosophy. So why not use them? I eventually produced a better product by not forcing my original idea. Honest self-assessments are crucial to your success.

It will take time for you to fully comprehend the scope of your ideas. Your mission may have a learning curve - which represents the changing rate of learning for the average Joe in any activity. The steeper the learning curve in your life design, the more detailed your plan must be. A steep learning curve means that the basics of your subject may be simple at first but become more difficult as you progress through them to higher levels of expertise. For example, most of us have a basic understanding of the functioning of our right and left brains. The right side is the emotional and creative side. The left is more analytical and linear. However, the more you learn about how the brain works, the more complex the subject becomes. Even neuroscientists do not fully understand every aspect of brain function. It is a subject matter like space; the more we learn, the more there is to learn.

By contrast, Level Three is difficult at first, but gets easier as you adapt your thinking patterns (applying meta cognition). It's similar to the learning continuum which states, the more you learn the more you can learn. It's not that you pile on more knowledge, but rather, increase your ability to acquire more.

Planning is forecasting. The writer Alan Lakein said succinctly, "Planning is bringing the future into the present so you can do something about it now." It's mapping. It's recognizing shortfalls and tallying the number and sizes of the bridges you will need to span gaps in knowledge or expertise. Planning is logic, and the development of the type of thinking that must be practiced throughout the process. Level Two gave you clarity of purpose. Level Three will give you clarity of function.

The function of the architectural plans is to show the builder a detailed schematic of the site, elevation, size, dimensions, depth of foundation, materials, wiring layouts, plumbing routes, structural design, facade, windows, doors, hallways, walls, emergency systems, landscaping and whew - floor plans, lighting, colors, direction, orientation, scale, legends, cutaways, cross-sections and well, lots and lots of stuff, vast amounts of necessary stuff. Nothing is pointless. Nothing is left to chance. Everything is designed and included to achieve the vision, to the highest standard of the project, with the best quality, in the shortest possible time. What does your plan include?

Your plan does not need to be literally drawn like blueprints, but you should think about your plan in terms of architectural rendering, of generating an image from an idea and then forming a cohesive plan to make it happen. Have fun. Use visual cues. Remember the big picture. Plot it out and then sort out the main themes. Ask the big question. What comes first? What type of due diligence may be required? Is this one of those unfinished projects? Where are you in the process? Your plan is an opportunity to learn, to grow, to adapt and to acquire wisdom to pass along.

Most architects design holistically, working in phases toward the overall design rather than compartmentally. Imagine that five architects were presented with the task of designing a resort hotel. Each one was given a different piece: the facade, the lobby, the overall size and layout, the exterior facilities and the entertainment space. What if they were to each design their particular piece, create the blueprints, hire the contractors and show up at the site simultaneously, without ever collaborating on the overall design? Obviously the project would be a disaster. Your third level must be a hybrid of sequential and holistic design thought processes. You must work in a logical fashion while planning ahead and making adjustments along the way. Your life design must be a fusion of emotional innovation and practical application. It's about learning to strike a balance between your heartfelt ideals and your resources in order to hit your extraordinary goal. This is how American Renaissance-Man, landscape architect, mathematician and musician, Paul Comstock explains it, "the real job is balancing the ethos of the conceived environment against the epistemology of building the thing. It a question of balancing vision, process and sequence. An exquisite landscape will do this. When people look at it, they will feel alive. The real challenge is, can you build an environment that will make any sentient being feel lucky to be alive?" Gosh if there is nothing else you get from trying something extraordinary; I hope you feel lucky to be here, able to try.

What Else?

Your plan must include time set aside for periodic updates, status checks, review and reconsideration for forward momentum, ensuring that you are working toward your goals and not veering off. Your plan is your sherpa, your Kato. It is essential to have and imperative to follow. Your plan may also surprise you by helping you to see errors in judgment or mistakes in time allotments. It may also help you discover new ideas or latent talents and opportunities.

A Japanese proverb tells us that a vision without a plan is a daydream.

Ayn Rand however, said "Throughout the centuries there were men who took first steps, down new roads, armed with nothing but their vision." We haven't yet heard from most of them.

You will need support for your life design from benefactors, family, loved ones and colleagues. Your planning will demonstrate your seriousness to them and make it easier to enlist support.

Explain your plan to your support crew in simple terms. Einstein said if you can't explain it to a six-year-old, you don't understand it yourself. Since that kind of logic worked for a genius, it should work for the rest of us. It will also help you learn to present your ideas succinctly, which will become important when trying to pitch it to a potential investor. Start enlisting support early on in the process. They may guide you, just as support columns can act as a means to find your way in a big architectural space. Your thoughtful plan will engender confidence and rally enthusiasm. This is the conversation at home without a plan.

"Hey honey, I'm finally going to make us a ton of money."

"That's wonderful dear. How are you gonna do that?"

"Uh...Well I was watching this show on the finance channel and I had an idea that, if I studied something like, ya know, nano-technology or animal husbandry, I could develop a new product and I could maybe get it on Oprah. That seems to work for most people. Like they say, it's not what you know; it's who you know."

"I'm going to my mothers. Clean the garage."

The man needs a little help on his elevator pitch. And he needs a plan. We've all cast blame on someone or something for things "not going according to plan." So we pout, curse and give up.

"Nothing ever turns out the way I planned."

Actually, things have gone exactly as you planned, lousy.

Without a plan we exist in what I call negative space. In architecture, negative space, or the shape of the empty space that surrounds objects, creates or encourages movement. In the realm of prosperity and abundance, a negative space creates restlessness. We develop a craving to fill that emptiness so we do for the sake of doing, without a clear purpose or an orientation toward a goal. Your impatience makes you jump from one quick fix to another and short-term solutions only drain energy and add to your anxiety. We spend money just to spend it (that makes us feel as if we actually have it - temporarily). We make hasty decisions about romance or business which leads to the failure that reaffirms our belief that, "things never work out for us." For things to change you must change them. Shape the space around you. Encourage movement and participation in the excitement.

Planning on the fly is for escaping prisoners not architects, and certainly not Level Sevens. Your plan must be all inclusive. We must consider the richness of the experience, the fun, the intellectual challenges, personal rewards, and the effect on our long-term philosophy. The plan must consider all factors, including; timing, cost, physicality, impact, aptitude, resources, originality, mentors, support mechanisms, training tools, and in the shadows, the Four Architects of Achievement. A word of caution; do not let this limited list limit your plan. Don't allow limited ideas to make you narrow-minded. These are preliminary categories. They are suggestions for chunking your plan into manageable sections.

Time Frames - Be realistic about timing. Nothing will frustrate you more than not completing your tasks by your deadlines. On the other side of that coin; things always take longer than you think. If you set optimistic, yet unrealistically short time goals, you risk anxiety and self-doubt. Confused? It's fine. Just do your homework and try to be realistic. For example; you can't obtain a real estate license in 2 days; it's a 75 hour course in most states and may be offered on a part-time basis to accommodate people who are working full time. It may take ten successive Saturdays to complete.

Don't set ambiguous time frames, like, 'soon after' or 'at some point'. Your plans are specific and mission critical. These are not things you're gonna do some day, they are the must do components of your process.

Your plan should include time to practice, to improve, and to master the chief skill you need to be an expert. It doesn't matter if you are planning to become a home renovator, a marine biologist, a ballerina or a single dad, what matters is your decision to be the best. Determine what is the most important quality you must have to achieve and sustain the project you are designing. The practice regimen you design will be organized when you set your success habits, which are the systems you will establish in Level Six. But the important thing is to incorporate training into your plan.

Cost - Are you investing in restaurant or a network marketing business? They have wildly different financial requirements and may require the securing of capital. Your financial estimations should include everything: computers, printers, paper, toner, books, licensing, insurance, education, transportation, tools and travel. No item should be considered insignificant. Consider financing for a major purchase such as a home or business space. Include interest and fees.

Making a drastic alteration to your life? Consider moving expenses or the costs of education, counseling, training, reading materials and seminars.

Physicality - Do you need fresh space for your project? Will you be clearing out a room, a basement or the garage? Consider borrowing space. The space will be determined by need and availability. Are you designing a workshop, manufacturing facility, a home office, writing environment, eatery, storefront or pet adoption center? Consider physical dimensions and limitations; work flow, efficiency, visual impact, and how the space is perceived upon entry to it. Will it feel like you're in the right place to finish your project? Will you need space for computers, blackboards, desks or counters?

If your life design is more geared toward changing your personality or repairing fractured relationships, think about clearing out clutter, reorganizing, resurfacing, painting or cleaning your living space, moving up and moving out. I am convinced that when I moved from a small one-bedroom apartment to a larger, brighter apartment in a nicer neighborhood, the open sense of space freed my mind. I literally had nightmares about my old building. When I moved, I felt better about myself in the nicer place and that helped me write a better book.

Resources - What is absolutely essential to complete each step of your project? Where are the best places to obtain information, tools, assistants, money, direction and help? Identify your resources by type: money, equipment, human resources (training, assistance, team members), and other types of support. Which of these are already at your disposable or which do you need to obtain?

Training, Education, Certifications – All of these elements will be completed on Level Five, in the welding of the core, but they must be planned for now, on this level. Find out what skills are required for your project and determine your current level of expertise. Maybe you have no acceptable level of proficiency in your field but always wanted to be whatever it is you've decided on. So what? Go for it. It's going to take some extra time, but you were only going to waste it otherwise, so be productive.

Determine what government agencies regulate your business. What are the licensing or permit requirements? How much are the fees? What are the prerequisites?

What type of training or mentoring will boost your confidence so you can rebuild your life? Which doors must you knock on? Include everything in your plan and incorporate them within existing time frames, adjusting as you add or subtract elements.

Some tasks can be completed simultaneously. Consider overlapping elements to compress time rather than finishing them in a strict sequence. Did you ever watch a house under construction? The roofers shingle while the plumbers rough in the pipes, while the landscapers remove boulders. It's the planning that makes this contemporaneous work a symphony instead of a fluster-cluck.

Tools – It's all about using the right tool for the job. Every carpenter, mason, electrician or other craftsman would agree. Learning to use the right tool for the job at hand is invaluable. What tools will make this task easier? Do you need upgraded technology or software? Do you need help preparing presentations? Are there experts that you can point, guide or direct your prospects to?

Impact – How will this affect family, personal life or friends? This is a list stopper for some people. People believe they are held back because of fear of failure. I believe the opposite is true. Fear of success is insidious. It has three prongs, each of which carries a different sting depending upon the individual: First, you may fear you will attain a higher level and then not have what it takes to sustain it. You may feel as though you've reached a level beyond your limits, so better to stay in a safe zone.

Second, you may feel you have propelled yourself into a position that you don't deserve. In 1978, clinical psychologists Pauline Clance and Suzanne Imes, termed this the Imposter Syndrome. It essentially means competent people sometimes can't believe in or accept their own competence. They think their competence has been thrust upon them by others who see them as more intelligent than they really are. Sometimes people who suffer from this believe their success was a matter of good fortune or timing, that they are frauds and don't deserve the success they are enjoying.

These worthiness issues are a more deeply seated but certainly fixable emotional problem, requiring a big boost of confidence that stems from your belief in your mission and support from your team. You must forgive yourself, for everything. Make your amends, and let it go. The hardest person to forgive is you. Do it and the forgiving of others is easy. To have prosperity you must cut the negative emotions loose and make room for the positive. It's alright to recognize the work you put in to achieving your level of success, whatever that may be. You were there. You took the risks and put in the hours, so you deserve it.

And finally, many people who go into business, especially women, fear the long-term costs of success, the alienation of peers, the disconnect from family (children) and the loneliness they may experience at the top. Men are not immune from this.

Fear of success is prevalent among those who are dissatisfied with their current lot in life. You are not alone with these thoughts. Sometimes we create an atmosphere of dread unnecessarily. It's always worse in our heads than reality. Talk it out with a trusted agent. You will find your fears will diminish when you let them out in the air. They shrink under scrutiny.

The personal sacrifices you will make will have an enormous long-term positive impact on your life and the people you share it with. You have to be committed to sacrificing the television, the paint-ball tourney and the Friday night poker games. This doesn't mean leisure time isn't important. Don't justify laziness by calling it relaxation. Real leisure is one of the elements in Stephen Covey's 'Important' quadrant. But the reason you sacrifice now, for the life of the mission, is so you can completely enjoy your leisure time when it won't pull you off course, when it is a reward instead of an escape. Your mission should be felt in your gut, something that's a part of you, a place you simply must build.

"Architecture is something visceral. It's something tangible and tactile. It's certainly much more about experience than it is about shape or even theory and ideas. It's an immediate art that provides reference, that clarifies relationships, that can reveal certain aspects of a place or activity that no other art can." - Brad Cloepfil

Aptitude - "Our genes are not our fate," proclaims Dean Ornish, a clinical professor at the University of California, San Francisco and founder of the Preventive Medicine Research Institute. He is a pioneer in the use of diet and exercise programs in the treatment and reversal of heart disease and prostate cancer. The changes in our cells and genes which are brought on by his healthful programs are powerful and they are accomplished in notably short periods of time. Growing clinical evidence in a new field of science supports the idea that we can improve the way our genes function. Some of us have lived with this misconception that we are born to a fate of mediocrity and only the lucky few have what it takes to accomplish meaningful change in their lives. Eliminate that thought. It's just simply not true.

Although our genes are basic ingredients of our structure and form, they do not predetermine the type of person we will become or our level of success. Our genes are expressed through factors like environment, habits, lifestyle, diet and work ethic. (This theory is explained in the work of K. Anders Ericsson et al, "The Acquisition of Expert Performance") We are all, it turns out, much more capable than we ever believed. Genes are ingredients, like flour, water, salt, oil, sugar, yeast and eggs. If I gave those ingredients to five people with different levels of baking skills and placed them in separate kitchens, each with a different type and quality of cooking tools, they would bake five very different cakes. It's not the ingredients, but how we use them and under what circumstances, that determine the cake which is produced. Our work habits and personal decisions ultimately drive the progress we make, rather than something as inconsequential as birth order. Once I learned this, it was disconcerting to think I may have squandered some productive years because I believed in my own deficiencies, but you can't move forward mired in regret.

The emerging science of epigenetics, according to Dr. Bruce Lipton, author of "The Biology of Belief", is based on the premise that our genes do not control our health and they do not control how we behave. "Conventional medicine is operating from an archaic view that we're controlled by our genes. This misunderstands the nature of how biology works." This is a strong statement, bursting with implications for the future of medicine and human behavior.

Epigenetics literally means "above the genome", meaning it is made of biological components (DNA methylation, histone marks etc.) that dictate how genes are expressed (behave). The markers that turn genes on and off are the architectural materials of our human buildings, our eye color, height, skin tone and a host of other physical traits. But they also determine our likelihood of acquiring certain illnesses like heart disease, cancer and dementia. Although it may sound counter-intuitive, both nature and nurture have implications for genetic behavior.

Time ran an article called, "Why Your DNA Isn't Your Destiny" written by John Cloud. He discussed biologists such as Joseph Ecker of the Salk Institute, who suggests that the epigenome is like software to your genome's hardware. The application of that software affects the way the genes function on the body's platform.

Lipton and other scientists from this field claim we can control epigenetics through our diet, lifestyle and behavior. If bad habits, such as smoking, can cause disease, then good habits can prevent or reverse them, but more importantly for Level Sevens, we have the power to transcend the misinformed limitations of our DNA. "You can rewire yourself," says Dr. Lipton. "You must recognize that you are a participant in the unfolding of your life."

Expertise in any field, as detailed in studies by K. Anders Ericsson in "The Genius Project" - has exposed the fact that true talent is expressed through a process called "deliberate practice". It is something revealed, something that is built, not something innate. Most of us are born with the capacity to learn just about any subject. We must identify our starting points and find the sources of information that match our level of understanding and progress from there.

Bill Downs, a nutritional biochemist and CEO of a company specializing in the development of gene-guided wellness solutions, told me that genes are like the keys on a piano, "It's how you play those keys that makes the music." Through epigenetics, the scientific world is learning that it's not so much what you are born with but the interplay of conscious action and the circumstances under which that genetic material is developed that have significant impact.

Let's use my son Jackson as an example of open-ended language capacity. We adopted him from Vietnam when he was 2 months old. He was born with the brain functionality that would permit him to learn to speak and write his native Vietnamese. But with that same functionality he could also learn any other language including English, depending of course on his upbringing. Today, at age nine, he speaks perfectly good American English and not a syllable of Vietnamese, but not because he doesn't have the ability. Had he been raised in Vietnam he probably wouldn't have learned much beyond a rudimentary street-market English, enough to sell souvenirs to tourists, but he would be fluent in Vietnamese. As a child he could have learned one language as easily as the other, even though they are drastically different in every aspect: phonology, morphology, semantics and structure. The fact is; it was the course of his life that determined which language he spoke, not his ability.

The neural mechanisms for learning language are like a computer with sophisticated hard-wiring but no software. The input of the language skills or the acquisition of those skills from family, environment and school are the software that is, in effect, downloaded to our natural hard drive ("Brain Research: Implications for Second Language Learning" The ACIE Newsletter, November 2001, Vol. 5 No. 1 - by Fred Genesee, Professor of Psychology, McGill University, Montreal, Quebec). Once we acquire language we can harness the processing power of the brain.

You may not know a thing about physics, but had you been raised by two physicists, you would certainly know plenty about the subject. The only law of physics I know is; nothing ever falls off the floor. And just like the language skills of little Jacks everywhere, it's not that you were incapable of learning physics; you simply weren't exposed to it. It's how you choose to advance that determines your aptitude, not your genes. Can we alter our biology? The science of epigentics is young, but the possibilities are staggering. Just a few years ago the National Institutes of Health funded 190 million dollars toward this research. That's no small investment for something of passing interest. This science is emerging and it is attracting attention.

This field has implications across a wide swath of qualitative applications, including the misunderstood and somewhat mysterious definition of genius. Consider that many, many moons ago, long before we knew that genes even existed, three intellectual men summed up genius this way:

> **Aristotle** - " Excellence is an art won by training and habituation. We do not act rightly because we have virtue or excellence, but we rather have those because we have acted rightly. We are what we repeatedly do. Excellence then, is not an act, but a habit."
> **Warren G. Bennis** - "Excellence is a better teacher than mediocrity. The lessons of the ordinary are everywhere. Truly profound and original insights are to be found only in studying the exemplary."
> **Alexander Hamilton** - "Men give me credit for some genius. All the genius I have is this. When I have a subject in my mind; I study it profoundly. Day and night it is before me. My mind becomes pervaded with it...the effort which I have made is what people are pleased to call the fruit of genius. It is the fruit of labor and thought."

Originality - Architects are always working between two forces that compete for prominence in the design. They are art and utility, also known as, form and function. They learn to adapt to and operate within the pressure of trying to be original in the creative design yet remain balanced against practical concerns. For example; how would you hide restrooms in an art museum so they don't detract from the product of the artists, while making access to them practical for the patrons who need to pass their lattes?

Always attempt to strike a balance for practical purposes, without sacrificing the creative talents you just worked so hard to develop. Don't be afraid of your own brain. Don't be timid about originality, but be careful not to force it. "Design is not making beauty, beauty emerges from selection, affinities, integration, love." - Louis Kahn.

Mentors, Guides, Friends -Are they the best or what? Contrary to what you might think, successful people are usually willing to share their thoughts on how they came to be successful. They have their own processes they've developed and we can all learn from their experience. What's wrong? Can't get that interview with Steve Wozniak? The Donald won't answer your calls? Try the library, the internet or your indie book seller. Read about great lives. Read memoirs, biographies and historical accounts. Find out who their mentors were. Learn from the experts, not your brother-in-law. Consider an apprenticeship. "Chance favors the connected mind." - Steven Johnson

Support Mechanisms - We all need them. The best contemporary architects work with other designers, planners, builders, contractors, graphic artists, modelers, accountants, drafters, aids, and their own education and experiences. Ask yourself this question, "Why would the people who can afford to spend weeks in Fiji as part of the Anthony Robbins Platinum Club, actually need to be there? Isn't their ability to afford that luxury proof enough of their success?" No, because successful people are always learning from other successful people.

A friend once told me he didn't believe in listening to people like Anthony Robbins. He said, people don't need life coaches; they should motivate themselves. Knowing my friend was a sports fan I asked him why they need coaches in professional sports such as baseball. Every team has hitting, pitching, base-running and position coaches, yet the players are pros, at the top of their game. Why should they need coaches? Shouldn't they know how to play well by now? Why do they get paid 4 million a year if they still need coaching? I'm still waiting for his answer.

The Four Architects – Like the stalwart Four Horsemen, these four principles will ride with you throughout your journey, and stand with you long after you move on to the next project. They are required patriots, bonded in solidarity with your mission. They are your crew, your posse, your Knights Templar of spiritual growth. The Four Architects of Human Endeavor are Vision, Courage, Commitment and Truth. All successful American endeavors have been buttressed by these principles.

The first architect is <u>Vision</u>, the utopian image of your life, your invention, your emotional turnaround or your business venture. The second of your flying architects is <u>Courage</u>, the stones to be different, to make a change, to step beyond the possible. The third patriot is <u>Commitment</u>. Commitment is the old salt of the crew. He has been through the battles and knows that a compelling belief in your vision, strapped with resilience to weather the dark days, will help you, above all the daydreamers, to see your mission completed. And finally, there is <u>Truth</u> - veritas. You must be honest with you first and equally so with your support team. You must be realistic in your plans and most importantly, true to your decision. Frank Lloyd Wright said, "The truth is more important than the facts."

Your four architects may be horsemen, warriors, soldiers or chefs. Imagine them any way you wish, as long as they are there. My four warrior architects are in khakis and black turtlenecks and they probably need haircuts, because it's cool to be a little wispy, but hey; they are armed with leather messenger bags jammed with pencils, protractors, sketch pads and million-dollar ideas. Don't laugh, these guys are resilient. OK, so maybe my design team doesn't evoke images of galloping shootouts with the Dalton gang, but my team is trained, accessible and driven.

Read the following passage written by Duane Lester of The All American Blogger and note how the Four Architects supported the president's decision.

"On May 25, 1961, President John F. Kennedy announced before a special joint session of Congress the dramatic and ambitious goal of sending an American safely to the Moon before the end of the decade. A number of political factors affected Kennedy's decision and the timing of it. In general, Kennedy felt great pressure to have the United States "catch up to and overtake" the Soviet Union in the "space race." Four years after the Sputnik shock of 1957, the cosmonaut Yuri Gagarin had become the first human in space on April 12, 1961, greatly embarrassing the U.S. While Alan Shepard became the first American in space on May 5, he only flew on a short suborbital flight instead of orbiting the Earth, as Gagarin had done. In addition, the Bay of Pigs fiasco in mid-April put unquantifiable pressure on Kennedy. He wanted to announce a program that the U.S. had a strong chance at achieving before the Soviet Union. After consulting with Vice President Johnson, NASA Administrator James Webb, and other officials, he concluded that landing an American on the Moon would be a very challenging technological feat, but an area of space exploration in which the U.S. actually had a potential lead. Thus the cold war is the primary contextual lens through which many historians now view Kennedy's speech. The decision involved much consideration before making it public, as well as enormous human efforts and expenditures to make what became Project Apollo a reality by 1969."

Kennedy had a vision, the courage to proclaim it, a strong commitment to see it through and a belief that he was impelled in the right direction. The four architects are always there, in whatever incarnation you desire.

So how are your plans coming along? Take heart that this hard work is worth it. Planning now saves you angst later.

Let's look at Phase II of your retail exercise:

The7th Level Imports – Phase Two of the Retail Exercise

Where will this store be exactly? Can the neighborhood provide the foot-traffic you require? What stores are around it? Will you have an on-line purchase option? How will you begin to acquire inventory? What will your price points be? Do you need to travel to meet your vendors and establish relationships? What wholesalers will you deal with? What are the return policies? What will be your store's return policy? What credit cards will you take? How do you set up those accounts? Do they require deposits? Do you need reserve cash on hand – how much? What licensing or permits might you need? How do you handle import taxes? Do I need an accountant? Do you imagine it on a busy street or more of a mall setting? (Can't help it - I'm from New Jersey)

How much inventory will you buy? How much money will you need to start? How much is the rent? What is the length of the lease being offered? Is it negotiable? How much must you gross monthly to stay afloat, to turn a profit, to pay your loan?

The table below represents one, simplified way to lay out your preliminary plans. Your own planning will certainly not match this neat format. Use it as a guide and be cognizant of the details.

Time Frames	Phases	Education	Work Product	Completion
Cost	Supplies	Tools	Space	Fees

Physicality	Location	Size	New	Clearing Old
Resources	$$$	Partners	Institutional	Tools
Training/ Education	Certificates	Schools	CEU's	Coaches
Tools	Physical	Technological	Out-sourced Pros	Expert Advice
Impact	On whom?		On What	Potential Gain
Aptitude	Self-Assessment: attitude, resilience, desire, integrity, character, principles etc.			
Originality	Style		Content	
Mentors Guides				
Support	Who	When	How	
Your Four Warriors	Vision	Courage	Commitment	Truth

More Basic Training

Here is a well-worn method for getting some extra stimulus for crafting your plan. Well-worn ideas work, in architecture and in life. Like they say in San Antonio, "Hey, if it works, don't fix it." So in keeping with the unbroken, the following stimulator list is in order of importance, beginning with the why, because if the reasons why you are designing your life are strong enough, you will make the effort to figure out how.

Why - Don't be shy - be honest.

Why am I doing this? Why do I need a change? Why do I have to try again and again? Is it for self-esteem, my children, my parents or my peers? Is it because I'm tired of living the way I am? Have I disappointed myself too many times and let down the people I care about? Is it my time, finally? Am I who I am and where I am because of the decisions I've made in my life? Am I in control of my own decisions? Is it finally time to knuckle down and write a real plan for my life? Do I want to contribute to the world? Do I want to leave good memories in the minds of my friends? Do I want to participate in my culture? Do I want to create something lasting? Am I the voice of abundance now?

What? - What if? What's missing? What is needed or necessary? What have I decided on? What color, size, shape, design, or method will it be? What tools, machines, or books will I need? What funds are available? What are the schematics? What is the name of my business or project? What materials will I need? What can I borrow or barter for? What material components will express the parti or value of my project?

If you are opening a small business, you should consider taking courses in small business management, or applying for free services provided by volunteers from the business community. You can have fun and make money too. Even the architects need to eat. Their business must be profitable to afford them artistic freedom.

Who - Who do I need to be to accomplish this? What changes must I make in my personality, behaviors, friends, triggers, habits, lifestyle or schedule? Who will be on my team? Who will be my supporters, mentors, trainers or guides? Who has the knowledge or wisdom I need? Who will embrace this idea? Who must I sell on it? Who will watch the kids? Who wants to be a part of this design?

Architects want to make positive changes to the landscape, the culture and the community, however, the essential goal of architecture is to actually build what has been designed, so they must collaborate with construction managers to discuss cost control, project scheduling, purchasing, documentation and field/site supervision. No matter how innovative an architect is, he or she must rely on teams of artists, critics, engineers and others to translate ideas into a real structure.

How - How long? How much? How often? How deep? How many? How critical? How will I accomplish each element of the design? How will I assess my progress? How will this affect those around me? How will I pull this off? How will I get the training or educational requirements I need?

Where - Where will the work be done? (school, library, basement, garage, Canada, or on-line?) Where will I set up shop? What is the best location for my project or business? Where is the best or most affordable school? Will I need to relocate, at least temporarily?

When - What are all my timelines? When do I need to start each new phase? When must I complete them? What deadlines are absolute? When will we open? When do I start looking for an agent? When do I ask for help? When do I need certificates, permits, permission or peer review? When does the first draft need to be completed? When do I start the process for securing finance? When do I review my progress with my support team? When will I finish the educational component?

When will I involve my family in my project? When will I forgive myself for my mistakes and stop allowing guilt to stop me from moving forward? When will I stop doubting and start believing?

Why not? - Why not dare to write a novel, invent a new building material, or invert a business model? Are you going to let four short words - "It will never work" - stop you? Really? It's that easy?

You may ask "why not" and then answer, "I don't know if I'm ready." You'll never be perfectly ready, so right now is always the best time to begin. Of course you may not be ready for every aspect of your mission, but you are ready to start the process. Don't worry about it. Jot a few ideas down in the blank table below, then after you finish the book, go back and complete it as part of your continuing work process.

Sonia Gil, the co-founder of the language software, Fluenz, was asked in an NBC interview about challenging the big language software company that owns 95% of the market share. She said, "Everyone at Fluenz is radically passionate, *passionate* about languages and I can sit here and say this confidently, nobody can do it better than us. And that's the bottom line." Her attitude is "why not challenge these guys?" our product is better. You have to admire her confidence.

Why	
What	
Who	
How	
Where	
When	
Why Not	

My Seven Levels

Level One

- Find a unique platform for expressing personal development.

Level Two

- Write a life design book inspired by architecture and run seminars based upon the book.
- Lay out the parallels in a simple format.
- Assign each level a central idea and appropriate analogy to architecture.

Level Three

- Decide who my audience is.
- Determine the voice of the book.
- Collect material from research into personal development.
- Explore scientific applications to personal growth concepts.
- Organize books, notes, articles etc.
- Write the book. (L5)
- Have it professionally edited. (L5)
- Research the competition in the field of personal development marketplace. (L5)
- Design the cover, layout, size, interior layout/format, font type & size. (L5)
- Determine which pictures or tables are necessary. (L5)
- Speak anywhere I can on the principles of the book. Consider advertising budget, target audience, media, length and style. (L5)

Level Four

- Inspire confidence in the program to help people overcome doubts.
- Be focused and organized. Make writing the priority.
- Resolve to continue **The Seventh Level** as a business process.
- Be honest in self-assessment of the work product.
- Generate a sense of urgency in my work life.
- Don't stress over things I can't control.
- Forgive - Forget - Forge Ahead
- Be a better father.

Level Five

- Study Architectural theory.
- Read the following: "Architecture" by Jonathan Glancey; "Why Architecture Matters" by Paul Goldberger; "101 things I learned in Architecture School" by Matthew Frederick; "Sketch, Plan, Build" by Alejandro Bahamón; "The Secret Life of the Grown-up Brain" by Barbara Strauch; "Idea and Phenomena" by Steven Holl; just to name a few. (The complete list is in the appendix.)
- Watch and read interviews with contemporary architects.
- Gather insight from the American Institute of Architects, the AIA and other go-to sources from the field.
- Actually write the book.
- Perform the following tasks as planned in Level Three: Have it professionally edited. Research the competition in the field of personal development marketplace. Design the cover, layout, size, interior layout/format, font type & size. Determine if pictures or tables are necessary. Consider advertising budget, target audience, media, length and style.
- Take speaking courses. Attend seminars to get ideas about style, length, format and delivery.
- Complete the project before I die of old age. (that's funny)
- Create a blog as a prelude.

Level Six

- Eat healthy and exercise at least three times per week. Eat a brain-friendly diet and take organic supplements.
- Treat everyone with dignity.
- Learn social-networking technology.
- Always carry a notebook or recorder.
- Never read or hear a principle of architecture without linking it to **The Seventh Level**.
- Stay organized with notes, background material and other data.
- Write every day.
- Always seek new media to write for.
- Know more about the architectural processes than anyone in the personal development business.
- Relentlessly pursue knowledge. Stretch my brain.

Level Seven

- Publish the book through a traditional source or find my own.
- Start working on a novel.
- Mentor my seven levels philosophy through blogs, talks, etc..
- Develop a merchandising plan for **The Seventh Level** related products.
- Design my own home using sustainable architecture.

Test Yourself - See if how far you can plan right now by writing notes for your own levels.

One	
Two	
Three	
Four	
Five	
Six	
Seven	

Almost Ready to Dig

I'll close the chapter on planning with a review and a look forward to your soon-to-be-defined identity.

Matthew Frederick says, "Being process oriented and not product driven, is the most important and difficult skill for the designer to develop." It's a concept I keep repeating throughout the chapters of this book. You need to enjoy the work.

Success is not always in the destination but the thrill of flight. It reminds me of the expression, "Getting there is half the fun." Architects learn the basics of their jobs in school and refine them over a career. When you build your levels, the process is less formal, but equally important. Keep in mind the some of the tenets of personal growth: life-long learning, an honest identity, the mastery of mission-critical skills and the opportunity to pass along your lessons. Getting better at getting better, is a reward in itself. Immerse yourself in the process, internalize it and enjoy it.

As you form your foundation in Level Four, you will shape the person that can rise to the task of accomplishing your design. You can look at it as retooling your identity. Some of you may just need some fine-tuning and not a complete overhaul. Whatever your case, you are designing your life for self-fulfillment, not self-aggrandizement. You are not seeking applause but abundance. You can share your methods for creating abundance and then more can be generated. It's not about feeling better than others but feeling better than you thought you could about your own abilities. It's not your flesh that needs sunlight, it's your soul. The MIT Press review of Robert Venturi's book, "Lesson from Las Vegas", indicates that Venturi "Created a healthy controversy by calling for architects to be more receptive to the tastes and values of common people, and less immodest in their erections of heroic, self-aggrandizing monuments." The Fourth Architect of Personal Development - Truth - will help you stay grounded in the mission, so you don't get swept away in your own brilliance.

Who do you need to become? Are you earning what you're worth? What kind of person lives this life, runs this business, teaches these kids? What are your work habits, behaviors, goals and mastery rituals? How can you improve your work ethic or become more efficient? What identifies you as the designer of your life? These are the questions in the platform of Level Four.

Level Four
Your Foundation

*"Society needs a good image of itself. That's the
job of the architect" -Walter Gropius*

By the time you've finished this chapter, you will be the best person there is to finish your project. You will create the platform from which you will launch your commitment to a lifelong disdain for mediocrity.

You have built your first three levels and your plan is in place. Level Four is bedrock. All things build up from this place, for you and for architecture. In order to construct a durable foundation that will support a large building, the engineers must dig down. No structure is built from the roof. The core rises from the base. In order to discover the best character of your being, you must excavate the old one. In order to be the best person to complete your design, you too must dig down, before you can build up. You must cart away the rubble and start fresh, level, and solid.

Civil engineers describe deep foundations as those formed to such a depth that their load bearing capacity is unaffected by ground-level conditions. Surface or superficial pressures do not dislodge the footings. Deeper foundations are designed to transfer the load to more competent strata if unsuitable soils are present near the surface. In level-seven-speak; having a deep personal foundation will help you bear potent loads. It will help you persist even when petty, incompetent, unforeseen, distracting surface soils, otherwise knows as negative influences, are pushing you into a state of instability. You are the bedrock now. You are the foundation upon which you will build your optimal life.

This is a critical level. It is broad-based and supports all the others. You must, must, must decide upon the person you need to be, not just to design your extraordinary life, but to live it. When you designed the first three levels, you identified your mission and your action plan, now you must identify the project manager. Who is it that will be the planner, the overseer and the doer? It's not as simple as asking what type of person can do this, but rather, *who* is this person? Who is this champion that leads this remarkable life? What's his story? What is he like? What would he never do? What comes to mind when you think of him? Imagine that this mission is already complete. What is it about him that makes it possible? Who is he at his essence?

An person's essence is what would remain if you stripped away the physical and superficial attributes used to define him. The French philosopher, Rene Descartes, expressed this concept with his wax theory. He demonstrated that a block of wax has certain observable physical characteristics that we use to define it as wax: shape, texture, feel, color, smell etc. Descartes said as you move this block of wax closer to the heat of a flame, those traits can change as the wax melts, yet it doesn't cease to be wax in our minds. The essence is what remains after the external attributes are altered. Professor Dan Ariely was deeply scarred by the heat of the explosion, but his essence remained to excel.

We make conclusions about a person's type every day at work, school and social functions. We seem to just know if someone is smart, ambitious, kind, cautious, angry, introverted, outgoing or a combination of myriad traits.

"Oh, I can tell that's the kind of guy he is."

"He is the type who would (yada yada) I just know it."

"She would rather wear a steel wool bra than go out with a guy like him."

How is it that without really getting to know a person, we can surmise their type? How do we draw these conclusions, and why do we seem to be right about them, more often than not?

We observe their conduct, their actions and we unconsciously note their tendencies. We compare how they behave in situations that are professional, adverse, uncertain, fun, volatile or sad with similar behavioral patterns of personality types we already know. These types have been established in our minds over our lifetime, from the thousands of interactions with everyone from baby-sitters to waitresses to colleagues. We have classified their various traits in our mental databases that we built from all our experiences back to infancy, back to mom's first loving smile. In short, we make judgments about people, often on little information, by comparing what we observe to what we already know. According to Professor Malcolm Gladwell; it's called thin-slicing. We do it all the time, in choosing mates, friends, business partners and in deciding which lawyer, doctor or political candidate will best serve our needs.

We observe their posture at parties or around children. We notice how they enter a room or where they sit in meetings or the classroom. We notice posture, eye contact, and countenance, but subconsciously we also register fleeting micro-facial expressions and subtle shifts in body language.

The developing field of biopsychology, attempts to demonstrate how biological and physiological processes interact with emotions, cognition and other mental processes. In simpler terms - it's how the stuff that happens within your body affects how you act. What you do with your body directly influences your posture, not your physical posture but your demeanor. Did you ever try to imitate someone's walk? You need to capture their persona to do it right. The beliefs surrounding the interconnectedness of actions, demeanor, personality and character are based on neuroscience, biopsychology and the mysterious behavioral complexities described by experts like Malcolm Gladwell, Paul Eckman and a host of others who inspire their work.

How does your personality manifest itself? How do your co-workers know what they know abut you? Why are some people restrained around you while others are instantly attracted to you? What tips people off to who you are? Do you seem to fit in to some situations easier than others? What cues are there about your level of comfort in a situation? Do others sense your authority? Do you seem at ease in your surroundings?

The answers lie in the observable behavior described above. The way we behave, consciously or not, is instigated by our self-image within a given context. People around us intuitively assess the congruency of our words with our actions and with the situation. Intuition is flash-cognition that happens on a subconscious level, but registers emotional reactions.

The question for Level Four is; can we reverse the process? Can we create a comprehensive list of the manifest behaviors of the individual who can achieve our mission? Can we then 'do' those observable things, in an effort to become that person who is what we aspire to be? Does conducting yourself this way over and over bring about lasting change? I think it does. Dr Lipton's research indicate the subconscious mind is built on habituation. it learns from patterns and the repetition of patterns. But to do it effectively you must have the critical factor of genuineness. You must commit to real transformation. You can fool others for a time but never yourself.

When psychologists look at the Big Five personality traits of openness, conscientiousness, extraversion, agreeableness and neuroticism, they make a conclusion about the type of personality you have based upon answering a long series of questions about your personality. For example, you might be asked to agree or not with statements about intro/extraversion such as:

- I like to attend parties.
- I start conversations.
- I keep to myself in social situations.
- I am comfortable with strangers.

You are posed dozens of these types of questions for each of the five main categories. Based upon your answers the psychologists develop an assessment of your personality.

What I want you to do is reverse the process. Build the personality by creating a bank of the traits of the person you aspire to be. How, you ask? You will answer list of questions as if you were that person. Your responses will define the traits for your personality bank, but the key is to imagine yourself as the person who actually does what you are designing. This is a real test of your imagination, so don't worry if you feel awkward in the beginning. As the data for your persona grows you will become more relaxed answering the questions. But you may even have to go through them several times to get it right. That's OK.

Just like a bodybuilder needs to change his routine to shock the muscles into further growth, this exercise is designed to shake up your psyche, to question yourself. Frank Lloyd Wright said to design from the inside out. In order to adopt your new persona, you must first define it. Don't define it in general terms such as hard-worker or type 'A' personality, but in blueprint detail. It's sort of a Socratic method of self-definition. You ask the questions and you provide the answers. Hey, you can't be marked wrong that way. In time the picture of who you need to be will come into focus, in much the same way as it happens when you interact with another person over a period of time. You do this every day, it's normal behavior. Just turn it around.

To build Level Four you thin-slice your best self, working the process at a deep plane. You will identify the patterns of behavior (habits, activities, mindset, demeanor, competence and style) of the person who is the ideal individual to accomplish what you wish, and then make the changes necessary to become that person. You may not need much, but small changes can have a huge impact. What would happen to a building if the first course of concrete blocks was just one degree off level? Don't disregard the little improvements. They become the foundation from which you will actually work the plan. This is mission-critical stuff. You must be the only person who could possibly pull off what you want to accomplish. If not you; then who?

Define it, accept it, be it. Over time you will carry your new self the way your new self ought to. The person you will become inside will be manifested in the way you walk, the way you articulate your ideas, the clothes you wear, the car you drive, the daily routines you develop. This exercise will help you uncover aspects of you that need prodding or flat out need to go. Socrates said, "The unexamined life is not worth living." He was not known for his sense of humor.

Levels Two and Three demonstrate the logic of your program, while Level Four represents your emotional commitment to it. That's why, in a sense, it is a treaty with the old self. You will create new canons of commitment and use them to keep you on course. This is a precise and permanent change in the person you've become comfortable with, but a change for the greater good. It is a pledge to excellence. Your drive will lift those around you. Your friends will feel your energy for achievement. It's magnetic, but only if you believe in you. "I know we cannot have great architecture while it is only for the landlord", said Frank Lloyd Wright. You must do for you before you can do for others.

Let's Define You

"The phenomenon of architecture is a development of the phenomenon of man." - Harold Bruce Allsop.

Listed below is an inventory of 150-plus questions to help you form a clear mental image of the architect of your mission. It's not binding and by no means all-encompassing, so you can adjust it to fit the needs of your project or the peculiarities of your self-expression. We are seeking optimal personal performance, by refocusing, arranging priorities or maybe just giving a lift to what's sagging.

It is your identity which will ultimately govern how you will pursue your plan and direct which course of action to take in response to any stimuli.

Focus on your mission as already accomplished. Think of a person you may know who already does what it is you want to accomplish. Or perhaps choose a well-known person who is the epitome of your adventure. Who runs this successful restaurant? Who leads this family? Who plays classical guitar this well? What kind of person is a general contractor, wine merchant, landscape engineer, pharmacist or programmer?

The questions are loosely organized into six categories: physical accessories, attitude, lifestyle, work ethic, philosophy and aptitude. Don't accept them as the only questions you should ask or feel obligated to answer them all. They are a guide. It is an exercise to guide you, not a test to fail, so loosen up. The big list of questions is written in first person because you are re-shaping your new identity.

The Big List of Questions

Physical Accessories	Attitude
What kind of car do I drive?	What makes me laugh?
What photographs do I carry?	What am I happy about?
What style of furniture do I like?	Am I adventurous?
What style of house or condo or apartment do I prefer?	Am I confident?
Do I concern myself with its architecture?	Am I energetic?
	Am I affectionate?
Do I live in a big city?	Am I comfortable in my own skin?
Do I wear jewelry?	Do I enjoy teaching?
Do I live in the suburbs or a rural area?	Am I a good listener?
Do I like history or art and architecture?	Do I think before I speak?
	Am I empathetic?
Do I wear a watch or carry a pen?	Am I tolerant of others?
Do I own a computer - what kind?	Am I sincere?
Do I have a smart phone?	Do I like animals – children?
What kind of shoes do I wear?	What does my handshake feel like?
What is my hair style?	To women?
Am I clean shaven every day?	How do I define happiness?
Can I tie a necktie?	Am I friendly to strangers?
Do I choose my own clothing style?	Am I affable and approachable?
Do I travel?	How do I dress when I'm home? For business meetings?
	How do I treat strangers?

Lifestyle	Work Ethic
When do I rise for the day?	Can I concentrate?
Do I meditate?	Am I a mentor? Do I have one?
What time of day am I most productive?	Who do I trust in business? Am I trusted?
Do I have any rituals?	What is the most productive use of my time right now?
Do I have a good memory? Do I carry a recording device in my car?	Who are my business heroes?
What are my television habits?	How do I dress for work? Am I punctual?
Do I bank on-line or in person?	Do I set goals - do I write them down - Are there long range and short term goals?
Do I shop for food as needed or at supermarkets?	Do I review my work after it is complete?
Do I recycle?	Am I honest with myself in assessing my work?
Do I write letters?	How do I handle professional criticism?
Do I like sports, competition, champions?	Am I comfortable expressing my creative ideas?
Do I like movies?	Do I enjoy public speaking - do I need to improve communication skills?
How much cash do I keep on hand?	What types of training do I have - do I seek?
Do I understand banking?	Do I have insight ability? Do I even know who Robert Sternberg is?
How much sleep do I require - how much do I get?	Am I an entrepreneur? Define it.
Am I generally healthy? Am I optimally healthy?	What is leverage?
Do I drink alcohol?	Am I punctual?
Do I draw or doodle?	Am I satisfied with my vocabulary?
How do I dress to go shopping at department stores or malls, errands?	What did I improve today?
Do I handle money well? Do I have credit card debt?	Am I industrious?
Do I have long-term investments? Do I manage them?	How much education do I have - how much do I require?
Do I remember my dreams?	Am I a productive autodidactic?
Do I write in a journal?	Do I work better in groups or alone?
What are my hygiene routines and standards?	What will I do in the next 90 days that is different from the last 90?
Am I a member of any organizations?	Am I committed?
How do I manage stress? How do I relax?	Can I focus?
What do I snack on?	
Do I burn candles or incense?	
Do I have pets?	
Do I exercise - before or after work - early morning? Define it.	
What is my diet like?	
Do I like music?	

Philosophy	Aptitude
Are there relationships that need mending?	Am I open to learning new subjects?
Am I religious/spiritual? Do I pray?	Am I confident in my ability to expand my brain power?
Do I vote?	Do I eat a diet rich in brain-friendly nutrients?
Do I consider world affairs?	
How do I define success?	Do I plan my week?
Do I have any guiding philosophers?	Am I action oriented?
Do I talk – really talk – to my children – partner - parents?	Am I inventive or innovative?
Am I close to my family?	Am I curious?
What am I proud of?	Do I believe you can work yourself smarter?
How do I define integrity?	Do I read books/magazines? What kind? What have I read lately?
What will be different about my life in 5 years?	What have I learned today?
Do I have empowering beliefs? Name 2.	Can I articulate my thoughts - in writing?
What will I never do?	Do I share my business/entrepreneurial ideas with my spouse?
Do I have heroes?	
What is my biggest obstacle to success?	Do I have past accomplishments?
What is important every day?	Do I enjoy the adventure of learning?
Am I honest in my personal assessments?	Am I capable?
What is significant in my life?	Am I willing?
What is character?	Am I enthusiastic?
Do I believe in destiny, karma, or fate?	Am I coachable?
Do I make the decisions that shape my life?	Can I think on the fly?
What is courage?	Can I adapt and overcome?
Do I have close friends?	What is my biggest asset?
Do I like my job? Would I change my profession of I could?	Am I earning what I'm worth?
Does my work affect the environment?	Am I creative?
How do I deal with obstacles?	
Am I proud of my accomplishments?	

There are no wrong answers, only what is reflective of the ideal person to lead your mission. Write down your responses in your workbook and refer to them as you progress into your project. You will need them again when you develop your systems in shaping Level Six.

When you are through you will have identified the type of person you must be to realize your dream life. You will have a profile of accomplishment. Once you've identified this person as the prototype to lead your project, once you recognize the persona that reflects your life, you will begin a sort of internal metamorphosis. This is your quest on the fourth level, to cocoon yourself in your work and emerge the better being. Start making the daily effort to behave the way this person would. Use whichever forms of habituation work for you: affirmations, meditation, checklists or Buddhist mindfulness. You prepared a detailed plan in Level Three, now be the person who can pull it off. Be the change you need to be. Be the person who is already doing what you envision.

What's that noise I hear? Self-doubt? Not sure if you have the intellect? Don't be silly; of course you do.

What is Smart Anyway?

Define it for me, right now. Smart is... What? A person who is smart is... To be smart means that you...She must be smart because she can...

Grab some paper and write down the qualities of the smartest person you know. What is it about them that makes you feel this way? What kinds of things do they seem to be good at? What sets them apart? Is it their behavior, their financial success, their ability to remember details, names or events? Do they seem to know a lot of trivia? Do they understand concepts easily? What makes them different from those who aren't as smart? What are their habits, their attitudes, their approaches to education and learning? Do they associate with other smart people?

Now look at your list and determine which of those qualities is a skill and which is a state of mind or attitude. What is their attitude toward new ideas, setbacks, stumbling blocks and curiosity? What is their attitude toward reading, television, enlightenment, spirituality and self-improvement?

You'll soon discover that much of what you deem to be their "smartness" is really about work ethic, priorities, scheduling, habits, commitment and perseverance. They stay with problems longer and they are eager to take on challenges.

I would suspect that most of what you perceive to be the qualities of a smart person are really the qualities of an industrious, goal-centered person. Sure they enjoy 'normal stuff' like movies and social interaction, but they also keep busy in other ways. They read books, magazines, newspapers and they read often. They watch educational television and TED talks. They see problems as opportunities. They articulate their thoughts well. They act on ideas. They are adventurous.

Some of you think a person is just born smart and that he or she simply has a bigger brain with more highly functioning neurons. In "The Secret Life of the Brain" Richard Restak, M.D., teaches that intelligence is not just about the raw number of neurons in a particular brain, "rather, intelligence has more to do with the number of interconnections among neurons. And the size and complexity of this vast network of interconnections varies at different stages of life and according to the challenges the brain encounters. When fully developed, the human brain's 100 trillion neuronal connections exceed those of any other creature on earth."

The human brain is the most sophisticated thing in the known universe. Its potential is limitless. There has never been a human being in recorded history who filled his brain to its maximum capacity and could no longer absorb another blessed thing. The smartest living person on planet earth can still learn another new concept before you finish this chapter, and do it every hour of every day for the remainder of her life.

Don't trust limitations - they always come up short.

Well what about skills? Is this smart friend of yours a wiz-kid on the computer? Is he good at brain-teasers? Is she a good reader? Do you consider yourself a good reader? If not, it's an easy fix. Anyone who is literate can improve their reading skills and gain the confidence to read more difficult material.

Reading is a complex skill according to Guinevere Eden of the Institute for Cognitive and Computational Sciences at Georgetown University. "In addition to linking letters to sounds, reading involves remembering the visual image of a word and memorizing its meaning. The beginning reader must also learn to sound out letters and remember those sounds as she decodes the other sounds that go with the word. Finally, as she reads the entire sentence she must remember every word so that when she reaches the end of the sentence she can put everything together."

Well gee, when you put it that way it does sound complicated; doesn't it? But you have already mastered this tricky reading thing, now all you have to do is improve upon the quality of what you read. How? Read more. Read freely. Read what you enjoy and read things you never did before. Don't force it. If you don't like it, put it down and read something else. Obviously you know how to read, but my experience in the work-a-day world tells me you simply don't read enough.

Some of you are confident of your cognitive abilities, while others may feel less so. Defining smart is ultimately about defining the issue, recognizing your shortcomings and identifying them as problems to be solved using your new architecturally centered brain. Builders and designers run into problems for a living. If it was easy anybody could design buildings. It's in the staying with the problem where the answers will come. Sometimes opportunity comes cloaked in adversity.

Can we literally work ourselves smart? You betcha. "If we were to employ a single word to characterize the human brain in all stages of development it would be plasticity: the organ's capacity to change. The brain's plasticity distinguishes it from anything else in the known universe. Without plasticity, the brain would be incapable of adjusting to changing times and conditions." - Richard Restak, M.D.

However, because of this plasticity, we can work our brains to develop or enhance almost any skill, even to advanced and master levels. Nobel Laureate Richard Axel describes plasticity this way. "If you use one sense or even a discreet component of one sense continually, and it is important for you, that indeed, the powers of recognition, the significance of that sense and, remarkably, the part of the brain that is devoted to that sense, expands in brain space. So a violinist, for instance, who uses the small fingers of his left hand for bowing, develops a region in his brain that detects the touch of his left pinky, that is far larger, three to five times larger, than the average individual.

It demonstrates the enormous plasticity of the brain; the ability of the brain to change the strength of its connections, the extent of its connections, to accommodate the unique requirements of an individual. And that affords us our individuality of thought and talent."

Science proves we can emotionally and physiologically alter individual attributes to accommodate the needs of the life design. Aren't you starting to feel better already?

The Whole "Rocky" Thing

On Level Six, you will develop the patterns of behavior that will eventually become habits of mastery. These routines will be part of your consciousness. They will be your true self. This is not an easy thing to do. Don't fool yourself. It takes work. It takes commitment. Hey; you're building a champion here so be patient. It's worth it, and so are you.

Why do we love champions like Rocky Balboa? Why do we route for them? Why do we get excited, whoop and carry on? Why do we cry when they cry? Why do we put our lives on hold to watch the Superbowl, the World Cup, the Masters, and game seven of the Stanley Cup Finals? What is it about living vicariously through the passion and drama of the competitors on talent shows that brings families together to see who wins?

Champions embody our aspirations. We tap in to their emotions. We feel triumph with them. We identify with them. I can't count how many times I have heard a sports fan use the pronoun 'we' when talking about his favorite team, "We beat them and we're gonna win the playoffs."

Internalize the feeling you get when you know you're watching a champion. I once saw Wayne Gretzky score a breakaway goal for the NY Rangers against the NJ Devils. The collective feeling in the arena was exhilarating as he broke from the pack, slicing through the ice toward the net. We knew it was going to be a goal. He knew it too. You could see the "Oh crap!" look on the goalie's face. He was toast. Those are life's fun moments in the company of greatness. Know the feeling. Own it. Be the champion of that little slice of life that you want to make extraordinary.

Paulie: How's your face?
Rocky: I don't know...how's it look?
Paulie: I wouldn't want it.

After you finish Level Four, go back to Level Three and ascribe your new personality and emerging ethos to your plan. "All fine architectural values are human values, else, not valuable." - FLW. See if the fourth level changes your perspective or your ultimate goal. If you must make a change, make an informed change, not one based on a whim. In his Pritzker Prize acceptance speech, I.M. Pei said, "The chase for the new, from the singular perspective of style, has too often resulted in only the arbitrariness of whim, the disorder of caprice."

In "100 Things..." Frederick points out, " If you rotate or skew a floor plan, column grid, or other aspect of a building, make it mean something. Placing columns, spaces, walls, or other architectural elements off-geometry because you have seen it done in a fashionable architecture magazine is a poor design justification."

Change for the sake of change or being different just to be trendy will not sit well with the newly defined you. Don't change on emotion alone - do what's right based upon your plan. If you make a change in an aspect of your character, do it for good reason. Don't change for the sake of change alone. You are crafting sustainable change, evolved to support your goals. Don't be who you aren't; be better than you can be. Keep looking to the architects for inspiration. Mark Sexton, in speaking of the role of architects in contemporary society, believes, "Architects have to be the great optimists. They have to be the visionaries. They have to look at what the world, and effectively, what man can be and we believe should be and create spaces and buildings that support that."

Although no permanent improvement can come without change, random acts of alteration will just muddle your life design. And remember what we said about fuzzy plans; they bring crappy results. At least that's what I think I said.

It's not always easy. Lasting change is built on commitment and habituation. It comes from truly believing in your capabilities, not just saying you do. According to psychologist Doctor Joyce Brothers, "You cannot consistently behave in a manner which is inconsistent with the way you see yourself." Gabriel García Márquez wrote: "Everyone has three lives: a public life, a private life, and a secret life." Guess which one is the most difficult to change? The way you see yourself (deep down in that secret place) ultimately governs the way you behave.

Bruce Lipton, PhD, points out that our subconscious programming often contradicts our conscious decisions, causing us to sabotage our own actions. "The major problem is people are aware of their conscious beliefs and behaviors, but not of the subconscious beliefs and behaviors. Most people don't even know their subconscious mind is at play, when the fact is that the subconscious mind is a million times more powerful than the conscious mind and that we operate 95 to 99 percent of our lives from the subconscious programs." This means that although you consciously push yourself toward successful ventures, there may be subconscious programming that's holding you back. This is why I said that part of digging your foundation includes clearing out the rubble and beginning from a clean base.

If you wish to accomplish more you must be more. If you wish to be creative you must create. You want to be a writer? Then get your butt in a chair and write. Set sail. Have a catch-me-if-you-can attitude. "I'm going - so come with me or get out of the way." Frank Lloyd Wright said, "No stream rises higher than its source. Whatever man might build could never express or reflect more than he was."

Architecture - A Cambodian Prison - A Four-Year-Old Boy

In Cambodia, torture is the primary tool of investigation, much as it is in 92 other countries. There are virtually no lawyers, the Khmer Rouge killed them all in the seventies and there aren't many who aspire to replenish the ranks. There are no investigators and there is no money to conduct a proper, thorough, legal investigation, like the ones we hope take place in our own country. Most of the people imprisoned in Cambodia are there for minor crimes for which there is no physical evidence of guilt, unless you count the electric wire burns wrought from torture-induced confessions. People spend many years in prisons like this across the developed and developing world, malnourished, beaten, and sexually abused - without ever seeing a lawyer or having a say in court.

But one little boy makes a difference in the lives of those prisoners.

In a captivating talk given by human rights defender and social entrepreneur, Karen Tse on <u>TED: Ideas Worth Spreading</u>, entitled "How to Stop Torture" Reverend Tse tells the story of Vishna, a four-year old boy who was born in a Cambodian prison, where he lives with his mother. He is loved by all, including the guards and because of this love he is given the freedom to move throughout the facility. This little boy, not even kindergarten age, tries every day to visit all 156 prisoners. He doesn't often succeed but he tries. Karen Tse says the prisoners look forward to his visits, that he is their sunshine, their hope, their greatest joy. Sometimes the visit is comprised only of Vishna poking his bony fingers through a hole in corrugated metal into a dark cell, followed by a friendly hello. Can you imagine how the architecture of his home influences his short life; the seclusion, the limited movement, the cold materials, the bars and the darkness? Even in an awful place, architecture directs one tiny destiny to deliver goodness. Karen Tse says of him, "Here is this boy, only four years old. He was born in a prison. He has almost nothing, no material goods, but he has a sense of his own heroic journey, which I believe we are all born into. He said, *"Probably I can't do everything, but I am one; I can do something. And I will do the one thing that I can do."*

Even though he is unaware of it, the architecture surrounding Vishna's life has an overwhelming control over his actions, his thoughts and his place in his personal history, much of which may never be written. You can be the architect of your own endearing life, one with positive influences, space to grow and a driving reason to improve.

So be everything you need to be to see this project through. Don't look back. The mere act of turning your head will generate doubt. Don't let it win. You win. You are valuable. You contribute. You matter, above all else, not because you are self-centered, but because the best person you are about to be is all your loved ones need for you to be. This is the beginning of the best part of your life. You are the foundation now. It's all about what you must do to get it done. It's not simply good enough; it's all there is. It's your life. You only get one. Make it extraordinary.

Level Five
The Structural Engineer

"Life is rich, always changing, always challenging, and we architects have the task of transmitting into wood, concrete, glass and steel, of transforming human aspirations into habitable and meaningful space." - Arthur Erickson

Level Five will be mentally and physically challenging, but satisfying in the end. This is the workhorse phase of the mission. Your foundation is set; now you have to build the thing. Whatever it is you committed to in Level Two, this is the time to get it done. Some of the work is already underway because for some projects the planning is part of the completed package.

By now you have clearly defined the 'why' of your mission and you have resolved to complete it. This is the hard part, the longest stretch of road. Sometimes the road will seem endless and you may lose site of the horizon, but take heart because you will look back on it with pride and exhilaration. During this phase you will learn the lessons that will guide you the next time around. You will learn efficiency, timing, flexibility and patience. These are the skills you will own, to use again and again. They are the ideals you will impart if you choose to be a mentor.

It's also time for a change in mindset. Until now you've been working like an architect, but now you need to work like an engineer. You have to exchange the black turtleneck for the white hard-hat. This is the heavy labor section, the core structure of your overall mission, an iron framework built to support the remaining levels.

Engineers work closely with architects for the detailed analysis of the design and then build the structural skeleton of the project. They are the elements that keep it upright, intact, whole and tolerant of built-in as well as external stressors. They do this with a surprisingly short list of essential materials, irrespective of the overall complexity of the project. Those materials include:

iron	steel
wood	reinforced concrete
laminates	heavy timber
carbon fiber	reinforced plastics
metal plates	masonry

They know which materials have proven best for specific applications and configure them in the appropriate dimensions to support the weight and stress of the building in conformance with best practices, manufacturer guidelines and building codes. Although the architect is ultimately responsible for the design, the engineers must work within the overall concept to determine which types of material to use based upon geometry, stiffness, span and load-bearing action. The engineers help design and build the unheralded but essential infrastructure: bridges, dams, pipelines and roadways. They are responsible for the planes, trains and automobiles that bring us neat stuff and help us get to fun places.

Architects move from a broad aesthetic (the vision) to a brouillon (rough draft), to the detailed schematics (blueprints). Engineers focus on specific structural elements, such as beams, to give the formation the stamina to span generations.

In the last few centuries the architect and the engineer have become distinct professions, due in large part to the complexity of design and the attendant physical demands of larger support mechanisms. Structural engineers are specialists, but in the past the architect and engineer were one profession. In this sense they were Renaissance Men. They combined their artistic and mathematical talents with their training in the trades and forged a single eminence as a master builder. We can work this way by overlapping disciplines as both the architect and the builder of our lives. This is your pocket renaissance, the new era of you; the quest for that elusive 7th Level.

In architecture and construction, the engineers are hired to ensure buildings can withstand loads; that they are serviceable, enduring, and won't collapse without warning. Engineers design structural elements that resist climate change, natural disasters and aging. They build based on historical knowledge and the laws of physics. This fifth stage is when the bones of the structure are set in place: the steel & iron, framing, beams, joists, cantilevers, columns and other modes of structural support. Concrete is poured, rebar is bent, rivets and welds are set. These steps create the structural integrity of the building. For us it is a time to define the aspects of your project that will drive the completion of your endeavor. Once you identify your drivers, you will place them as permanent residents at the top of your daily command list. Level Five is where you will apply your due diligence to the project.

You have a distinct list of drivers determined by your mission. They may include such tasks as your schooling and obtaining certifications. They may be the acquiring of licenses, permission and professional assistance or contracts. They may be the research, outlines and chapter notes for finally writing that novel, which may further include: interviews, historical and geographical research, plot lines, character development and of course, putting the damn thing down on paper. [Getting published may require a secondary 7-Level plan, but you can handle it.]

Your drivers are the critical action components of the final design. It is not the finished product, it is the work product. For example, drivers are:

- Your writing of a business plan
- Your purchase, corporate training and opening of your franchise
- The opening of your restaurant, the hiring and training of staff, the planning of the menu
- The lessons for your instrument or new language
- The manufacture and distribution of your invention
- The reconciliation with your family
- The production of your redefined identity for a career change

From this point forward, every book you read, every paper you research, every person you learn from, collaborate with and each completed step from your plan is another steel beam, another slab of timber, another lag bolt in your overall structure. This level is light on theory and heavy on action. Every element works together to build your castle.

Architectural splendor comes as the elements interact. Think back to what Professor Restak said about remembering moments as a manifold of individual pieces - like in a relaxing November evening at home. Fire up Samuel Barber's "Adagio for Strings" and imagine your Lisa Kristine print hanging over a reclaimed mantel above a Colorado-stone fireplace rising from the cypress floors bracing the charcoal walls and you will begin to feel the comfort of losing yourself in Cormac McCarthy's words while savoring a Paul Hobbs cabernet. Fill in the background with the snap of the fire, the hishing of the autumn rain through the cottonwoods. Now that's the way to be alone.

The beauty of your small successes is their interweaving, their collective contribution to the whole. One of the acquaintances I made while writing this book is the almost pathologically patient artist, architect and furniture designer, Roy McMakin. He reckons the challenge of pleasurable work this way, "What I most enjoy and find the most intriguing about creating architecture (as an artist with no architectural training) is the tension between the thing being created being both an object and a choreographer of the experience of living. I think good/great architecture has to have those things in balance. And, the other fascinating aspect of architecture is its relationship to providing service to another person (client). I think the only way to get the choreography part of things right is to find the right empathetic place to be with a client (which can be interpreted loosely)."

Artists and architects understand that sometimes collaboration serves to elicit better ideas. Often their ideas come from seeds sewn in another context. This strength-thru-community concept is why artists tend to herd in enclaves and downtown districts.

It's the interlocking of your levels that gives them their strength. Your levels are not disconnected stages that mystically form a complete picture in the end. They are purposely designed with the idea of pulling in the next one, like coupling railroad cars.

The engineer's job is to build a structure that can bear up to pressure and movement that may cause fatigue, cracking, shifting or failure. A supporting structure must do two things that reinforce the concepts of stones two and six: it must permit the architectural beauty to take shape and it must protect the systems that will be set in place so the structure functions. The engineer builds internal structures that perform under complex conditions, resisting both static loads (the mass of the building pulled by gravity) and dynamic loads (shifting and lateral forces). To attain the 7th level you must work through the complete process as planned and build something solid, but remain prepared to adapt to the unexpected.

All your creativity, planning and self-assessment, come in to ride with the Four Warrior Architects as you stand in preparation to hoist and weld your fifth level into a muscular core. You have the confidence to rely upon whatever you have built inside you to be sturdy enough to tackle the real doing of the project, to withstand the tension, bending and compression of the timber you have brought to uphold your magnum opus. As the engineer of your life design, you will build a structure that transfers loads to the solid foundation of you.

Adopting Kinetic Architecture

Architecture in motion is a moving idea. It's not enough for architects to create fantastic buildings, they want to animate them as well. In kinetic architecture, considerable portions of the building move without compromising structural integrity. It is movement with purpose. The building doesn't remain still; it can adapt to internal or external influences, such as shifting light, changing seasons, privacy or openings to the sky. Think retractable stadium roofs, rotating restaurants or if you would like to see some residential ingenuity, check out Alex DeRijke's Sliding House in Suffolk, England. Engineers must design these moving parts to withstand wear and tear, torque and mechanical failure.

I use the example of kinetic architecture to highlight the fact that you should remain flexible within your production environment. On Level Five you may need to modify your original plans. Once you begin the work you may realize there is a particular aspect of the plan that you were blind to. You may also discover something about your personality or have a change of heart about your end goal. For example; you might return to school to study civil engineering and find you have an interest in landscape design. You might enroll in culinary school and discover a hidden talent for creating desserts. Now instead of opening a restaurant, you opt for a small specialty baked goods shop. These are not problems just altered resolutions. You should work with your strengths and do what you find you love. Tweak your plan accordingly and press on.

Venezuelan architect/writer Ana Manzo relates kinetic architecture to humanity by stating, "There are already many constructed buildings that show us the advantages that this architecture brings in many areas of life: green design, space saving and many, many more. Here, no matter if the movement occurs on a small or large scale, the important thing is to produce positive changes in someone or something, either the inhabitant, the planet or both."

Shifting Winds

Good architects must learn to stay nimble, to react and adapt as complications crop up, such as structural challenges or last-minute concept changes from the client. They learn that things will not always go smoothly and changes must be made. They may have to consider options quickly and respond with innovative solutions; it's the choreography Roy McMakin spoke of.

I needed this attitude when writing the manuscript for this book. I would be naive to assume I created the ideal method to solve any problem or to plan all human endeavors. I didn't. It's just a template. I learned that I couldn't force it to apply in all situations so I had to adjust the book's tone. In working your project, you will experience setbacks and doubts. You will face distractions, interruptions, interference and purveyors of doom. Things will happen; it's inevitable. But, how we handle them will make the difference. These blips are signs of opportunity: to review, evaluate, refocus or pull a gut check. The work and ultimately your final project may not be everything you envisioned; so what? It's the human component of design. John Ruskin said, "No architecture can be truly noble which is not imperfect."

Matthew Frederick goes on to remind us, "When complications in the design process ruin your scheme, change - or if necessary, abandon - your parti. But don't abandon having a parti, and don't dig in tenaciously in defense of a scheme that no longer works."

Whatever path you choose to remain on, be the best. Have fun and work hard. Be flexible, fluid and agile. Be good at the little things. Frank Lloyd Wright said, "It is just as desirable to build a chicken house as to build a cathedral."

Consider this. Some people like graphic arts while others like creating characters. Some people do voices and some write funny stories or snarky dialogue. Some like overseeing artistic productions and some like managing temporary work sites. Whatever their specialty, the people I just noted collaborated to make enormously entertaining animated movies - "Shrek, Ice Age, Monsters Inc. and Puss in Boots."

It doesn't matter what you do, but by making the effort to excel you will always find a place to participate, an opportunity to be a part of something incredible. You don't need to be the hero, just a part of the action. Over my 25-year career in law enforcement, there were a few times I experienced what I call epimoments, (being at the epicenter of a powerful moment in time), those flashes in a lifetime when deep in your emotional furnace, you realize you are a part of something larger than you, something profound, like assisting in the emergency response center after the attacks of September 11th, or planning the inspector's funeral of a fellow officer killed in the line of duty; when dignity, honor, courage and compassion ring true in your gut.

Whatever your mission, wherever you journey, whatever it is you have chosen to be the best at; it is worthy of your effort because it will pull you out of the death-rut. It will lift you to where you can see more difficult challenges, and inspire you to conquer them. Whatever it is doesn't really matter so long as you do it well. And if you feel you can't go it alone then join forces with kindred souls to make it the best it can be.

The Professionals

If your mission is commercial then wherever possible, you should use professionals to make and market your product. Sometimes you just have to pay for lawyers, manufacturers, branding experts, agents and graphic artists. These people have already reached a 7th level in their field. They have the training and experience to guide you through unfamiliar territory. Their expertise is an invaluable tool. Use it. What's the point of writing a great book if no one reads it because you refused to get an agent or insisted on designing your own cover? Why invent the world's best coffee brewer if you can't get it in the stores or wouldn't invest the energy of due diligence to protect your intellectual property? Yes - you are a great baker - but you may need some help getting your first wave of customers through the doors.

There is a cognitive bias called the Halo Effect. It means if someone is gifted in a particular activity we assume they are proportionately talented in other undertakings. We erroneously believe one talent leaches into other fields. It works in the mirror too. Sometimes we delude ourselves into thinking we can do everything and that our own talents apply across fields we have no business playing on.

Hani Rashid talks about his profession being a compilation of expertise, "Architecture, I've always thought of as kind of a hybrid of other disciplines in some way. It's obviously a multi-disciplinary environment we work in and I sometimes liken it to the fact that we call on experts to give us structures or to give us acoustics or to give us sort of certainties in space, and those are normally called engineers. At other times we go to experts to give us metaphysics, to give us poetry, to give us, you know, emotion. And we will call those experts artists, I suppose. And I've always seen our role as some kind of an interesting hybrid of those two disciplines." Like an orchestra with unrelated parts producing a symphony, experts rely upon other experts to effectively express the grandeur of their vision.

Books sell in part because agents bring them to the right publishers, who know the marketplace, although this particular case I worked with a hybrid publishing house. Editors correct errors and help to enjoin voice with content. Graphic artists work with publishers to produce a cover that speaks to the core of the book, while captivating the guy who is drifting through the book store. I don't presume to know anything about these aspects of the writing business, so I entrust my manuscript with the professionals.

Do you really know everything you need to bring your product to market? Do you know if that nifty gadget you invented is best manufactured using the extrusion process?

"The what process?"

Exactly my point.

Architects aren't carpenters. Hockey coaches aren't strength trainers. Inventors aren't patent attorneys and writers aren't...well, writers are a strange bunch.

So use the professionals to help you whenever possible. You won't regret it as long as you check them out first. Again, due diligence pays off.

Sidebar

Don't dismiss something that could be useful simply because it's ugly. Its very ugliness might be what creates its utility. Take rebar (reinforced steel bars) as an example. Rebar is heavy, rusty, dirty, twisted, rough and can rip your skin apart, but it is critical in reinforcing concrete and other masonry structures. Its rough edges give it the bite it needs to anchor it to the surrounding concrete. As you build your core structure, you may need a gruff professor, a wily attorney, or a friend who practices tough love to help you anchor your new identity to your growing ideas. Like the t-shirt says, "Put your big-girl panties on and deal with it."

There are plenty of aspects of architectural necessity that are not pretty, such as elevator cores, fire stairs, storage areas, maintenance floors and boiler rooms. Things that are mundane are necessary for us to enjoy the whole experience. It's important to the overall practicality of the scheme. As you look across the atrium from the mezzanine of a spectacular hotel lobby you don't think about the steel that's keeping you from crashing eighty feet into the fountain but thankfully, someone did.

It all matters in the overall project. You are in search of total fulfillment on Level Seven. You won't be satisfied unless you fight some battles, overcome some obstacles, learn valuable lessons and inch closer to mastery, knowing that what you've built is enduring. The finished product only feels good because of what you went through to build it. So even though you're tired, the gratification will transcend fatigue.

So get tired. Work some long days. Lose some sleep. Need a haircut. Miss your friends. Forget the dog's name. Forget to eat! This is what you fretted about on the first two levels. This is what you planned for. This is what you wrestled with your soul for. Fire up the laptop, get out your homework, lace up your boots, turn on the stove, get in the classroom, and study, invent, create, write, build, sweat, cry and enjoy the glory of a hard week's work.

What's the difference if it takes five days or five months? It takes what it takes. This is why you planned, so that you will know what is necessary for the process, despite the grind. David Bly said, "Striving for success without hard work is like trying to harvest where you haven't planted."

Cue the Mayans...

What can the Mayan astronomers teach us about architecture and patience?

The Mayan culture reigned for over 2200 years, roughly from 2000 BC to 250 AD. Among the remarkable achievements of this pre-Columbian people was their accurate knowledge of astronomy, the movements of planets, the natural calendars and the changing of the solstices. They built observatories out of stone. The windows were aligned with the movements of the sun, the moon and Venus, to permit sunlight, moonlight and shadows to light up opposing walls. Many of their temple doorways aligned with the orbits of heavenly bodies.

They were remarkable. With crude tools, in ancient times, with no telescopes, no computer models, no CAD design and no written records of architectural or engineering procedures, they built planetary observatories by hand, with precise mathematical equations they developed themselves. So how did they know the exact manner to build these structures to allow proper observation and spiritual alignment? Patience. They stood outside at night and observed the movements of the larger celestial bodies. They tracked these movements night after night, month after month, year after year, with tools no more sophisticated than sticks and shadows. Over many years of practice, calculation and documentation, they designed scientific observatories, pyramids, government buildings, temples and calendars, which stand today as marvels of innovation and intellectual prowess. They quarried and moved local limestone into place, cut to the proper sizes and shapes, without draught animals, heavy equipment, and pick-up trucks. They did all this with ingenuity and brute strength. They took their time. They worked hard.

Sure there are those poetic champions of the working stiff like DH Lawrence, who wrote, "You'll never succeed in idealizing hard work. Before you can dig mother earth, you've got to take off your ideal jacket. The harder a man works, at brute labor, the thinner becomes his idealism, the darker his mind." No one ever said there is nobility in 40 years of lower back pain. But hard work with a purpose is noble. It stirs your heart. It enriches your existence. Ditch-digging is mindless hard work. Grave-digging is selfless human work. Both jobs make holes in the ground. One hole is filled with a daughter, a father or a friend. It is filled with a lifetime of memories or the haunting frustration of a child who never became a boy. The other hole is filled with a pipe. It's all about the purpose.

I'm not big on sports heroes, but one of my favorite lines about work comes from the greatest leader in team sports, Mark Messier, and what is particularly neat about him is his humility. "My jersey hanging from the ceiling is going to be a symbol of the hard work of those I played with." And my siblings would disown me if I mentioned Messier without Gretzky who said, "The highest compliment that you can pay me is to say that I work hard every day, that I never dog it."

But since this book is inspired by architects, I must conclude with this passage. The Louisiana State University (LSU) School of Architecture displays a unique first-person perspective of their program on the LSU web site called, "Arch a Day in the Life." This section is from the Third-Year Undergraduate Student - "Before I entered the architecture program, I was a business major. I went to class, went to parties, and got decent grades. Basically I had the typical college experience. After a year of this routine, I realized that business was not for me. After speaking to a friend who was an architecture major, I decided that design was something that I would enjoy. I was spending all of my time outside of class working on my studio project. After being on campus from 8:30 A.M.-4:30 P.M., I would stay in the studio and work on my project until about 4am. I was able spend so much time doing schoolwork because it wasn't "work"; it wasn't reading and studying, and figuring out the correct answer. It was a creative process that involved defining the problem and coming up with my own solution. Professors challenge us to explore not only different ideas and forms, but also to analyze our entire outlook on the world and to respond to it. I would push myself to create a design that I was proud of, and the best part was that there was no "correct" answer. I would come to studio and see all the different designs and approaches to a project. I saw that architecture was not just the cookie-cutter houses in my neighborhood. Projects get progressively more complex and demanding with each semester. I have learned not only technical issues, but I have also learned to manage my time better, and to evaluate my surroundings in new ways. Professors continue to challenge students to bring their projects to the next level. Architecture has given me a drive to push myself and produce something that I can be proud of, a drive that I couldn't find in any other curriculum. The architecture program has a strong community within the school because it has its own building and we spend so much of our time with the same people. Because of this, I have become close friends with most of my classmates. It is this community within the building, which makes committing so much time to working tolerable."

The lesson is simple - do what you love, do it well, do it with passion. But don't just try to find one passion; do everything passionately and the thing you do best will unfurl itself.

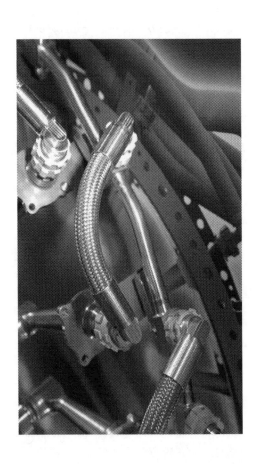

Level Six
Systems of Achievement

"Genius is personal, decided by fate, but it expresses itself by means of system. There is no work of art without system." – Le Corbusier

Architectural longevity is realized through the alliance of design philosophy and two sets of systems, those needed to build a structure and those required for its extended operation. Architecture is functional art, but it will not and cannot function without the systems built in to sustain the structure. The systems maintain what is created and afford us the luxury of enjoying the space, without consciously concerning ourselves with the weather or wondering if there are adequate supplies of power, water, air and light. We should only notice these things when they are awry.

After the skeleton of a structure is built, systems are put in place to preserve the entire building and properly control internal mechanical operations. Mechanical systems such as electrical, heating, cooling, plumbing, ventilating, fire protection, water supply, storm drainage as well as cable and fiber optic lines are installed and protocols are established to maintain them, in accordance with the wishes of the client, the demands of the structure, the needs of its occupants and the regulations governing their function. Properly functioning systems support the underlying utility of the architectural splendor. Regular repair and maintenance schedules are established to keep the mechanical operating systems working properly.

Some systems are designed to maintain specialized environments such as in museums, zoos, aviaries, aquariums, botanical gardens or homes and restaurants with live animals, ponds and display-size fish tanks. There are systems to keep the food fresh for the animals, to keep their living quarters clean and free of disease, and containing systems (fences, walls, cages) to protect the animals from harm while keeping us from being eaten. Systems create spectacle like the outdoor shows at the Las Vegas grand casinos. There are other systems fashioned to support our food supply, such as irrigation, crop rotation, climate control, forestry, population and pest control, along with bio-engineering and production. Systems have been established to move that juicy red pepper from the farm to the market to your salad, such as packaging, shipping, refrigeration, railways, trucking, pricing, and port management.

Systems are reviewed for their impact on building form, cost and efficiency. Without these physical systems in place and the maintenance procedures that are continually monitored and upgraded, the building will deteriorate. The pipes will freeze or rot, the toilets will overflow and the big screen presentations will fail. The outside elements will come in, and not in the good way like fresh air and sunshine, but in the bad way like rain, moisture, mold, carbon dioxide, excessive heat or cold. The experiences we came to enjoy will be spoiled. Disrepair will lead to disinterest and disgrace.

The National Geographic channel created a special called "Aftermath" in which they describe what would happen to the world if suddenly there were no humans. They explained in stark terms what disasters would occur if no humans were there to monitor the safety systems of nuclear reactors, oil refineries, zoos or warships; how quickly dairy cows, our pets and creatures in the city aquariums and zoos would escape or die, and how, over time, buildings, monuments and cities would decay. In one episode the producers demonstrated how a skyscraper would collapse on itself in just over a hundred years. As windows broke and roofing fell into disrepair, rain would get into the building, seeping down into minute cracks in the concrete - cracks which under normal circumstances would have been repaired by maintenance crews. Eventually water and carbon dioxide would ooze into tiny openings, finding their way to the rebar, which would rust. As the rebar rusted it would expand, causing larger cracks. Soon the structural integrity of the building would be compromised and beginning with the top floors, which see more rain etc., the unsupported weight of the building would lose its prominence to gravity. Under this scenario massive buildings would collapse floor by floor and in the ensuing decades, the remnants would be absorbed into the earth.

It is a provocative series. It demonstrates just how important systems and the people who operate them really are. Building systems provide services, such as drinking water and toilets, but more importantly, they preserve the physical structure so it can perform its function for many decades to come.

Listed below are two examples of work systems, the first is a small-scale operation and the second is much larger, but both systems must be followed or money and jobs could be lost and people could get hurt.

#1 - At the Restaurant

Imagine you are a kitchen manager. You and your team are preparing for the opening of a large commercial restaurant. You are tasked with devising a cleaning schedule for the wall & floors, every fixed area, stations, tools and equipment. It's a daunting job, but consider the impact on the restaurant's operations, reputation and income if the kitchen were to be shut down because of a health code violation.

Your first job is to consider what needs to be cleaned and chunk them into categories:

- Exterior - storage, delivery bays, doorways
- Interior - ceilings, walls, floors, storage rooms, walk-in refrigeration, employee bathrooms, dressing areas, office space
- Work Areas - Stock, dishwashing, prep and cooking
- Stations - vegetables, sauces, seafood, baking, fry, grill, sauté, salads, dessert, head cook, expeditor, etc.
- Equipment - fryers, stoves, ovens, ranges, hoods, broilers, refrigerators, scales
- Tools - pots, pans, plates, tubs, knives and other utensils

Next you would have to determine cleaning frequency:

- After each use
- Hourly or twice per shift

- After each shift
- Every 24 hours or every other day
- Weekly - monthly

In the third step you would establish the standard for cleaning each item. Should it be: swept, wiped down, rinsed, washed with soap & water, or sanitized etc.

In the fourth step you would decide who is responsible for cleaning each item and which types of cleaners/sanitizers shall be used, and who inspects items for quality control.

Finally, you must formulate a training regimen for rotation, schedules, chain of command, quality control, cleanliness standards and adherence to state and local sanitation laws.

All this and you haven't yet cooked a single burger. But if you consider that one small item, neglected for even one shift, could be the source of a food- borne pathogen that could cripple your business, you would be judicious in designing your system.

2 - At the Seaport

Unless we're in the Merchant Marines or worked at a seaport, most of us never consider the enormous task of unloading and reloading cargo ships.

In just one shift, upwards of 1600 heavy steel containers may be moved, presenting dangers to the crew and pressure to operate within limited windows of time. It's an enormous undertaking that cannot be accomplished without experienced personnel operating under strict systems and regulations.

As the seven-million dollar Gantry cranes offload containers, others are replacing them in a high-stakes balancing act. Place too many containers on one side of the ship and it could roll over, not only causing tens of millions of dollars in loss and damages, but potentially killing crew members. The hooks alone on the cranes can weigh as much as eleven tons.

At the seaports, hundreds of men and women use systems to track and orchestrate the movement of ships and containers, and the trucks who remove them from the port to distribution centers, where other systems are in place to unload the containers and truck the shipments to their final destinations.

Despite the pressure to move containers quickly, thirty per hour and more, well-established saftey precautions are strictly adhered to. There is never a disregard for safety and accidents are rare.

Systems and the people who operate them are crucial to the safe and efficient movement of cargo. Without them in place, goods are misplaced, fresh produce spoils, ships back up in the queue, money is lost and people get hurt.

Architects have systems as well, although they are more aptly described as habits. They are: progressive thought, attention to sustainability, life-long learning, staying current (with materials and building innovation), exploration of varied applications, broad-spectrum education (arts, humanities and sciences), collaboration, perspective and mastery. The rationale behind seven levels is to help you recognize that these architectural habits are directly applied to human endeavor and should be entrenched in your life as safeguards to what you will design. These patterns of successful behavior eventually become not just habits, but the essence of your core competencies. On Level Six you design routines that sustain what you have built. These are your systems of achievement. Like the physical systems in a built environment, they help to preserve what you have constructed.

Sustainable Architecture

The term sustainability is prevalent in discussions of architectural design. It is spoken of as frequently as craftsmanship and utility. Sustainable design refers to the type of architectural planning that is conscious of the environment in philosophy, function and the building materials. The processes of sustainable design are meant to enrich the environment and not leave it bereft of hope and resource. The building materials are retained from sources that are sustainable, renewable, recycled or wherever possible, have a limited negative impact on the environment. But Steven Holl cautions, "That greenness is not architecture in and of itself; something more subjective and more poetic that brings all the manifold parts and pieces together."

Sustainable design ideology considers future generations of users. It seeks to edify students of the processes that went into the projects, considering not just environmental but social sustainability in the foreground of thought. Terms such as well-crafted, sound, permanence and stewardship are important to your overall life design. Beyond the physical systems of a building, sustainable design also incorporates the consideration of the 'enduring quality' of the design. It is a philosophy of forward thinking.

Your life design systems must accomplish three objectives: first, they must support your design in a structural and evolving way. Second, they must progress from a conscious knowing of what needs to be done into an unconscious doing - the habits of triumph. And third, they must sustain not only your project but the character of your design, the prolonged existence of your newly formed philosophies.

Habits

Habits are behaviors that we repeat so often that they progress from conscious to subconscious acts. They are a part of who we are. Habits can be bad of course, like smoking and nose-picking, but good habits once worked into the subconscious, become inseparable from your character. They become the behavior patterns that others observe as influencing or representing your successful lifestyle. Daniel Libeskind says habits are shackles, but he is referring to creativity. I agree that it's good to break with tradition, think radically and unburden yourself from the provincial. But don't confuse the issue. The habits we are discussing here are work habits, habits of productivity, efficiency and continual improvement.

In Level Four we spoke of being able to judge someone's character by their behavior patterns. On this level you will begin the daily routines that will permanently dye the fabric of your consciousness.

You can start right now with your first assignment; the ideal time for action is in the very moment of your idea, your epimoment. Put down the cupcake, call your mother, do a push-up, cut your toenails and drive to work without flipping someone off. Do one small act in the name of progress. Each endeavor begins with one humble step toward maximum effort. How do you eat a hippo? One bite at a time, but they probably taste awful. In small but growing increments you enjoy personal fulfillment. You can acquire a sense of your own style, your ideal life, designed by you. You can have what you seek, without losing the ones you love in the work.

Wake up ten minutes earlier each day for one week to enjoy your morning coffee rather than slugging it down in the car. It will have a beneficial effect on your blood pressure and you will discover that being on time for work is indeed possible. And while you're at it, drink less coffee and drink more water. It helps your system run more efficiently. More efficiency means less need for stimulation. I didn't believe it either until I tried it. Take those extra few minutes to eat a better breakfast and no, toaster pastries do not count. After a successful week give yourself a little pat on the back. You can be more productive than ever in middle age so let's start giving those Gen-exers a reason to admire us. The small rewards help you maintain focus and beat back the natural tendency some of us have to be a little lazy.

You should define your habits by group, such as overall health, diet & exercise, education, planning, interpersonal relations, professional relationships, professional and personal development, goal-setting and mentoring. Some of these will be put into the subsets of daily, weekly, and quarterly routines. Precisely how you devise your personal systems will depend largely on what you are designing with your levels, and how you envision your future. Take the list below as an example of things you should be doing every day and then custom-make one for you.

Your Daily Operations

- Having mind over mattress
- Stretching, engaging the day
- Eating a healthy breakfast, drinking water
- Writing in your journal
- Reading something inspirational or reviewing your notes for ten minutes
- Following your plan for the day
- Making time for important things every day (family, education)
- Improving your craft in a push toward mastery
- Adding books to your must-read list and actually reading those books
- Checking in with customers, associates
- Seeking better customer relations
- Writing a quick note to an old friend
- Calling you parents
- Meeting other professionals

- Evolving, improving core skills
- Volunteering, meditating
- Following a balanced diet with supplements and vigorous exercise.

Your periodic habits are those that keep you on course. They are like the regular maintenance schedules of buildings.

What is your thinking like? Are you ferociously chasing your dreams? Are you character and goal centered? Are you learning to work more efficiently? Are you thinking in terms of sustainability? Have you made time for talking with children, checking on parents, knowing your children's teachers, knowing their friends, improving your personal library, and most importantly, getting regular medical check-ups? One of the reasons women outlive men is that they are in the habit of going to the doctor regularly, so they catch problems before they become irreparable. Men shun the doctor because we fear they will find something. We should hope they do, so it can be fixed and we can fall asleep without health concerns. The flight attendants always tell us to put the oxygen mask on ourselves and then help the kids. Take care of yourself so you can be strong for those who need you.

Healthy Brain - Wealthy Life

Barbara Strauch, author of "The Secret Life of the Middle Aged Brain", and Dr Richard Restak - "Mozart's Brain and the Fighter Pilot", both relate the essentials for continued brain growth and brain health, well into middle age and beyond. You must do two thing: challenge your brain and feed it well. If you want to tackle difficult projects or develop the confidence to learn new or more difficult material; you need a healthy brain. If you want to avoid dreaded degenerative brain diseases like dementia and enjoy lifelong learning, then you must have a healthy brain. Daniel G. Amen, M.D., author of "Change Your Brain - Change Your Life" and "Use Your Brain to Change Your Age" said something that I found startling, "The quality of the decisions you make are a direct reflection of the health of your brain." Just think about what that means to people like me who offer advice for personal growth. Without a healthy brain, none of this matters. So when your are drawing your blueprints, remember to include a nutritional plan. Unknowable factors can have an effect your decisions, so why not stack the deck in your favor? We can't control all the external influences, but we can control the person affected by them.

I suggest you read these important books, which are written in an easy, accessible style, so you can demystify your hazy ideas about how your brain actually works and how you can help it work optimally. The three most important factors in increasing sustainable brain life are:

1. Exercise - regular in routine and varied in type.
2. Nutrition- specifically a leaner, plat-based diet rich in fruits, vegetables, lean protein and anti-oxidants, and with a heartfelt apology to the great State of Texas I concede that steak is not very good for the brain.
3. Cognitive Stimulation

1. Exercise - 30 minutes of aerobic exercise three times per week, with moderate resistance work to keep bones and muscles strong. All blood flow is good, so the more we can increase capillary blood flow to places like our hearts and brains, the better off we are generally. At rest your brain uses 10% of your oxygen intake; but when it is mentally active, it uses a whopping 50% of your O2. This explains to the confused manual laborer how the office manager can possibly be so exhausted at the end of his day.

2. Nutrition - Fruits and vegetables are great but which are ideal? The darker the better: blueberries, strawberries, spinach, spirulina, oranges, kiwi, red grapes, broccoli, Brussels sprouts, cranberries, whole grain rices, etc. Realistically, most Americans eat a lousy diet and need supplements to bridge the gap between the way we should eat and the way we do eat. There are a number of companies that use nanotechnology to formulate their supplements. Nanotechnology is a much more efficient delivery system that increases the bioavailability of the vitamins, herbs and minerals. Organic and nano-encapsulated supplements are backed by real (published/peer reviewed) science, and are vital for the body's natural bulwark against disease, the immune system.

In studies supported by nutritional biochemist Bill Downs and Kenneth Blum, PH.D., "Nano-encapsulation is undoubtedly a more efficient and effective means of nutrient delivery, but there is still a cherry to add to the top of this proverbial ice cream sundae of revolutionary medicine. That cherry is something called increased bio-availability. A nano-encapsulated supplement requires less active ingredients than a traditional supplement or pill, and yet, still performs better. To put it simply, you get more and waste less allowing for a larger reserve of medicinal compounds and nutrients for those who need them."

To put nutrition in a seventh-level perspective; architects are always looking toward better products, newer materials and innovative methods to improve their craft. We must do the same to have the stamina to be creative and productive. Without a sound and virile biochemistry, we lose some of our drive to improve. It's all part of a holistic approach to personal growth.

3. Cognitive Stimulation - read more often and with more variety, especially after exercise. There is evidence that aerobic exercise ignites neurogenesis, the growing of new brain cells in the dentate gyrus (an area of the hippocampus responsible for things like memory). It generally occurs within 60-90 minutes of exercising. So why not go for a 30 minute brisk walk, take a shower, wash down a healthy shake and some grape seed extract and then read or study something new. Some of the scientific evidence, Dr. Strauch points out, suggests that these new brain cells are ripe for new connections, so to my way of thinking, the ideal time to learn something is after you exercise. Professor Dean Ornish recommends this simple program for optimal lifestyle:

- Diet - low fat, whole foods, plant based
- Stress Management - yoga and other spiritual based meditations
- Moderate Exercise - walking just three hours per week increases neurogenesis (the growing of new brain cells)
- Smoking Cessation
- Psychosocial Support Groups
- Supplements

Read material that challenges your conventional manner of thinking. Studies have demonstrated that the act of working to form cogent arguments - such as those you would have while reading material you might disagree with- can stimulate the brain to form new connections and make your brain function better. In northern Europe, studies of children raised in homes in which children are permitted to intellectually challenge the conventional wisdom of their parents, negotiating things like curfews, are less likely to succumb to destructive types of peer pressure. This is in part because this challenging and negotiating forces the children to be creative and form convincing yet differing points of view. They learn to think for themselves.

I have several friends with whom I disagree with on one subject or another. When we have our collegiate discussions we try to outwit each other or struggle to find common ground. It makes our friendships deeper, and our brains sharper. You should work to create a more demanding intellectual environment to live and work in, one that doesn't settle, one that explores, one that seeks a more complete understanding. This adds honor and credibility to your convictions. It's how you get to the truth.

And finally, I recently purchased the **Fluenz** Spanish language package for several reasons:

- Learning another language later in life is a great way to challenge the brain.
- There is no rush to absorb it all. Since there is no sunset date for fluency, I can work to learn it over a life-time. I can incorporate it into my regular routine along with exercise, a brain-friendly diet, reading and daily writing. Studying Spanish will become a part of who I am and how I live and a relaxed attitude will actually help me learn faster.
- It will help me while traveling to research my next book.
- I admire the business savvy of Fluenz co-founder, Sonia Gil.
- The format makes learning a new language fun and interesting. I highly recommend it. (no writers were hurt in the making of this shameless plug for Fluenz.com)

Homework

Today's homework is in three parts. "Did he say homework?" Yes, homework.

(1) This is a list of 50 words you should know the meaning of, not because they are germane to this text, but just because. You will see them in print somewhere along the way and it will serve you well to know them. Words represent concepts. The more words you understand (really understand - including their origin) the more concepts you

understand and the easier it is to navigate thru new material. You will understand more of the news articles and periodicals you read in the doctor's waiting room. You will try new things. You will understand the subtle complexities of things you used to skip over. Get a fat dictionary and start working. Improving your vocabulary is an important part of your bigger brain routine. This is a good start.

hegemony	quiescent	prerogative	amalgam	conundrum
aggravate	insular	seminal	subjective	acrimony
restive	qualitative	nonplussed	titular	sanguinary
visceral	supposedly	abstract	indemnify	paradox
ensure	irony	sacrosanct	laissez-faire	palisade
redoubtable	geocentric	dilettante	obfuscate	purport
iterate	inculcate	fortuitous	extraneous	corporeal
anathema	infamy	opprobrium	litany	travail
temporal	banal	fetor	harbinger	macerate
resolute	kismet	bollix	evanescent	gadzooks

(2) Continue the practice of metathinking. Put on your science-babe thinking glasses. Challenge the way you currently think. Notice how and when you generate your best ideas. When are you most stimulated? What kinds of attitudes, beliefs, rants and philosophies get you fired up? Think with energy. This is the beginning of the best time of your life. You have it all running in sync: the energy, the ideas, the youth, experience and your profound purpose.

Focus on one thing at a time. Attention is limited, say psychologists David L. Strayer and Jason M. Watson, "The premise of finite attention is now a cornerstone for contemporary cognitive neuroscience, and today it is well accepted that attention is limited in capacity and can be flexibly allocated among concurrent tasks." Think of focus as a bank of ten lasers (the number is arbitrary). You can train all ten beams on one target or five each on two targets or two each on five. Break them up as you will; with each division you have fewer lasers in your arsenal.

Strayer and Watson say "devoting more attention to one activity necessarily implies taking it away from others." They explain it as "knobs on a dashboard", amplifying some signals (facilitation) and suppressing others (inhibition). "Tuning attention appropriately is key to healthy cognition." (Scientific American Mind - March/April 2012).

(3) Be the new cerebral superhero, Plastic-Man. Remember that plasticity refers to the ability of your brain to adapt to environmental stimuli. Your brain needs stimulation; it's like driving a BMW - if you leave it parked in the garage it runs poorly. You need to drive it. Working your brain is like working a block of clay - you need to get in there and move it around, slap it and flip it over it to warm it up before you can sculpt something striking. Do something different. It doesn't need to be life-altering, just different. Watch a foreign film, grow a Bonsai tree, read about Buddhism, refinish a book case, learn to tie knots, find Argentina on a map, or just spend 18 minutes reading about a subject you know nothing about. And while you're at it, listen to Aaron Copland's "The Promise of Living," The title alone should inspire you.

A Daily Systems for Writers

1 - There is no system for writers.
2 - Every writer has routines, habits, fetishes and styles, and not one of them could function using the system of another. Some are regimented, others are haphazard. Some work crazy long hours and some are downright lazy. They all do what works best for them and wouldn't change a thing.
3 - The more I read about the daily habits of journalists, poets, novelists and biographers, the more I realized writers are a profoundly idiosyncratic mottle of talent.
4 - They are us, all of us at every turn- the hermit & the networker, the caffeine-addict & the drunk, the idealist, the nearly insane, the curious & the scholarly, and always the raconteur.
5 - They have one thing in common - they have to write.
6 - A system would only confine them.
7 - But for me; I did improve upon my filing, safeguarding of sources, organization skills, syntax, grammar, minimalism and other work routines that made me a better writer, or at least more productive.

OK, so writers weren't a good example. The point is, if we think of personal growth as a place or structure, we will plan to maintain it and improve upon it. We maintain the aesthetics and the functional aspects of our home. We want it to look appealing and we want it to work well as shelter. We often improve the systems as technologies advance. We upgrade landscaping or alarm systems, install new windows, paint, remodel and make repairs. We can take the same approach with our bodies and minds. Ask what aspect of your design requires annual maintenance. What must be inspected, evaluated, altered and improved? What must be in place permanently?

Write down your daily strategies of operation. Follow them until they become unconscious acts. Level Six is about systems, not affirmations. They are vital, not cute. Without systems buildings fail. Without your own achievement systems you will surely regress and you don't want to go back to where you were before you began working so hard. You've made a decision, so ride with your four warrior architects and stick it out - forever. Falling down hurts; staying down kills.

Scaffolding

Scaffolding is a temporary construction built to support crews, material and equipment to perform a function on the exterior of a building or in large interior spaces. They are made around the world from a variety of materials such as steel, aluminum, composite and bamboo. Scaffolding was used in ancient times to build large structures, such as temples, fortresses and palaces. In Japan, regulations require that large building undergo regular repair or maintenance. Entire buildings are surrounded by scaffolding every 10-15 years to conduct the necessary work. The scaffolding may stay erected for a few weeks to several months. This keeps the buildings in good operating condition so they remain viable for many generations. It's used every day in all types of construction. You can't walk five blocks in mid-town Manhattan without moving under or around some sort of scaffolding. From time to time, you may need to erect scaffolding to make repairs to or perform large-scale maintenance on your life endeavor. This is not a setback, it's to be expected as part of the overall process.

Think of scaffolding as a small-scale 7-level project, one that you can build to repair a portion of your life that has slipped in to disrepair, such as physical fitness. It's easy to get wrapped up in your life and career and then neglect your health. By thinking in architectural terms, you relieve yourself of dropping the ball. Just create a plan to get back on track. Build your temporary structure, fix the problem and get back to business. It's not a dramatic event or a reason to feel inadequate. Scaffolding is simply part of the business of an architectural mindset. It's a system to draw upon to assist with upholding the larger structure of your life design.

Mastery Systems

The highest degree of personal systems management is that which lifts you to mastery. You made an emotional commitment on Level Four, and now you will devise the mastery systems to raise your efforts to a plane beyond expertise. Terms such as master's degree, master craftsman, and Tae Kwon Do Grand Master, all invoke an image of something or someone to revere. It says with certainty that we are in the presence of a lifelong commitment to being better than the best which has culminated in this supreme level of achievement.

Some of your systems are meant to maintain viability. The next echelon of systems are designed to elevate, to enlighten, to embolden. They must be designed with the knowledge that they are a component of lifelong learning, of a relentless pursuit of regular improvements. Nobody becomes a master without devoting time to getting better. There is no such thing as quality time. That's just a goofy phrase invented by overworked single parents to make them feel better about neglecting their children. The only quality comes from actually spending more time with what and who is important. You have to be tenacious. Even architects, as brawny as their brain function is, are not regarded as masters until they prove themselves to peers and critics over many decades packed with innovation and production.

According to K. Anders Ericsson and his colleagues, attaining real mastery of a skill, such as, playing classical guitar, designing buildings or being a shortstop, may require 10,000 hours or more of sustained, deliberate, focused practice, over a relatively condensed period of time. Talent seems to be something less natural and more nurtural (no way that's a word). If so-called 'talented' people possess more of a champion quality than the rest of us, that quality would be perseverance. What Ericsson calls "deliberate practice" is not simply doing the same thing over and over; it's practice with purpose. It's the resolve to get better and better, setting higher levels of expertise with each benchmark attained. It's about failing to hit those benchmarks and then practicing until they are hit. Practice, perseverance and diligence worked in concert to push you to elevated levels of achievement will unearth your true genetic potential. Remember; genes are only ingredients. You've got to work the recipe.

Habits are bricks. Desire is mortar. Two bricks together begin a process. One brick becomes a course, and then a wall, and then a building. They become a place to create, to indulge, to parent, to learn, to achieve and to dream of more places. They don't appear through mysticism; they arise from vision, planning, diligence, patience and productive habits. You don't need to become the best at everything. That line of thinking will create frustration. So ask yourself what particular aspect of your life design, once mastered, would elevate the entire package. What specific skill should you master and how will you go about organizing a plan for this challenge?

I hesitate to discuss mastery because I am afraid you will lose the inclination to try new ventures or to continue your exploration of a diversified life. You may have built a beautiful boat of hand-cut reclaimed timber, adorned with a captain's chair made from Ernest Heminway's favorite bar stool, but you've got to take it out on the water, find some hidden coves, hit a few waves, scuba dive, land a black marlin (then release it please). One of the neat things about architecture is the variety of levels of artistry, craftsmanship, innovation, engineering and material use, that can be investigated in pursuit of peak performance.

With so many options, it seems incongruous to be so laser-focused on a single issue or subtle refinement that you miss the possibilities within the spectrum of learning. It's about balance; it's about designing mastery systems that allow for a free expression of explorative ideals. You can fall into a rut of sharpening one tool to such perfection that you never use it or forget you have other tools. It's the open mindset that got you here in building Level One, so don't let go of your inner seeker. In her paper entitled "The Cook, the Prospector, the Nomad and the Architect", Jeanne Gang of Studio Gang Architects, said, "This trajectory of fine tuning (which some would call fetishizing) lacks curiosity, the willingness to be surprised, the thrill of bold experimentation, and the chance to make a discovery. The accomplished master is in many ways no longer allowed to explore because his clients expect him to repeat and refine specific forms and details—years of polishing a single groove create a furrow so deep that escaping it is often impossible."

However, a commitment to mastery blows away a swipe at mediocrity. The push toward mastery will, like all heartfelt endeavors, have rewards in the process. Each step toward mastery is an individual accomplishment. Each action is another frame in your story. Your quest for mastery, by its existence, by its own parallel consciousness, will move your story into the extraordinary. Envision your mission at the master level and set a plan in place to achieve it. Ask this simple question as you work your plan; what do I have to do each day to develop mastery?

Just don't make yourself nuts obsessing over it. It's important to set high personal standards and work hard for your goals, but equally important to find balance. Limit the frustrations you create in your life. Don't spoil the fun of the original endeavor. In your quest for mastery it's important to remain curious. Don't let a single focus constrain your safari brain. Be open to new ideas, new perspectives, new barrels of talent that are stored right in your own cellar. Flick on some more light switches and go find them. But by all means, if you discover something you love doing, attack it like you would a break-away goal for the Stanley Cup. It's yours. Don't stop skating. Don't look around. Don't look back. Don't pass. Just focus, drive hard and score.

Looking Ahead

The systems used to create architecture are not mechanical. They are fluid and organic. They express themselves over time as new solutions are proffered, tested and employed. The systems fit the needs of the project as envisioned by the architect and determined by the complexity of the program and its scale; by the skills of the architect and the aptitude (size and talent pool) of the firm. One universal system doesn't apply to every project. Your systems are determined by your own needs, the drivers of your extraordinary mission, by their context in your life and your personal development milestones.

Make your systems work for what you desire. Don't try to force your life into some intricate, draining set of rigid systems. You must design them to sustain what you've built. You wouldn't build a manufacturing facility and then determine what products it can make. You would build the systems around the needs of the product design, the demands of the consumers and your forecast for expansion. Write your systems to serve your needs and to honor your quest for mastery.

In the next chapter we will discuss legacy. Does your extraordinary life matter? Have you added something to the lives of your children or other people? David Chipperfield believes, "The critical thing is to make sure that architecture is in the service of something. But I believe that's true whether it's your house or a museum. I'm nervous about architecture being the center of the stage, instead of being the scenery. Good architecture creates a place within which things are done. If one just said, 'well, what's important is life,' then architecture is not important. It's the life inside, then that might suggest that you don't need to bother."

Of course we know it does matter, and we do need to bother. Implicit in what Chipperfield is expressing is that we must build with a knowing that the life inside is ultimately more important than the trappings that surround it, that the structure we design and work to build, glorifies that life.

Level Seven
The Accidental Architect

"The idea drives the design, but the real test of architecture is in the experience, the moving through space, the overlapping perspectives." - Steven Holl

After the countless hours of tireless work, the ten-thousand phone calls, conferences, changes, delays and missteps, the building is at long last, finished. The architect will mount up and trot off to create anew, tipping his sketch pad to the weepy critics before sunset. It's time finally, to open the architect's inspired building and for its occupants to start working at the function for which it was intended. In these last few days the staff will put the polish on the conference table, buff the floors, fill the tanks with tropical fish, present the artwork, clean the carpets, fluff the toilet paper and install the furnishings. It's like the opening of a Broadway musical. You can just feel the buzz in the air.

For you it's time to complete the last walk-thru, to joyfully throw open the doors to your finished project and celebrate this extraordinary life you have designed. It's time to begin advertising your service, introduce the new you to the world, shop your completed manuscript to an agent, sell your product to wholesalers, send out resumes or hang that "Open for Business" sign in the window. It's a feeling you will never forget because of the emotions and sweat equity you have invested in it. This is what exhilaration feels like. Soak it in, savor it, smile openly. Own the feeling so you never doubt yourself again. But don't settle into the hammock just yet; it's also a time to review. Level Seven has three main elements: best practices, mentoring and satisfaction.

Did you achieve what you set out to do? Did you answer your <u>why</u>? Have you added value to your life and added even more to those who supported you? Did you ever guess, when wondering what you wanted to be when you grew up, that you would create an architectural plan to carry you through to your destination? Could you have imagined what the process would be like? Like Steven Holl says about architecture, "The real test is in the experience." So... how was your experience? Was it so much better than just thinking about it? Annie Han says the experience of seeing something real rather than looking at the drawings is what is deeply inspirational, "The potency of architecture are three dimensional experiences that are; it's built. It's like a real-life experience. You get to occupy the space." So your actual experience is much more compelling on a primal level than just your ideas, lingering in the wouldn't-it-be-great stages. Now you can say you 'got' to do it. The ideas truly pale in comparison to the doing of the thing.

It was fun, admit it. You didn't think you could pull it off, but something satisfying happened, something a whole lot better than boring. Through imagination and effort you became an accidental architect. Not the kind who gets huge contracts for designing skyscrapers, but the kind who works a creative process, who acts on ideation. You stumbled across this book and developed a system that just might help you find a little greatness inside you. You get it now. You understand the true meaning of process, diligence and expertise. Robert Hull of the FAIA says, "It's that process that almost becomes more of the craft than the finished product."

In architecture, interesting spaces are frequently created accidentally by the reorientation of the grid, or by random arrangements of focal points and furnishings. "Exploration is the real key. We've all been involved in projects where sometimes the anomalies are more important than the original idea. They're accidents." Says Tom Kundig, a Fellow of the AIA, "and you happen to be there on the site when they happened. The craftsperson might have even wanted to eliminate it or change it." But the architect says let it be, recognizing the kismet, the fortuitous nature of the event. During your journey you may have accidentally discovered latent talents or tendencies. You may have had revealing or even startling moments of self-discovery. These are good architectural consequences of being imaginative, of working through the process. It should feel damn good, but you have one more level to achieve in this system.

Level Seven is the critique of your work and the rendering of what you learned from the experience. Answer these questions: How did I do? What could I have done better, faster, more thoroughly? What have I learned to do more efficiently? Did I smash my biggest obstacle to success? Do I have the confidence to try something bigger and bolder? What have I learned about myself? What have I learned that I can pass on to a friend, a colleague, a loved one, or my children? Will my ideas, my perseverance and my lessons live beyond me, through my kids or those I teach?

John Ruskin said this about building to last. "When we build, let us think that we build forever. Let it not be for present delight nor for present use alone. Let it be such work as our descendants will thank us for; and let us think, as we lay stone on stone, that a time is to come when those stones will be held sacred because our hands have touched them, and that men will say, as they look upon the labor and wrought substance of them, See! This our father did for us."

When your children are grown and look back on their lives; what story will they tell of their dad? What did their dad impress upon them? What legacy did he leave the family? What did you build that they will want to tell their children about?

Mentoring gives value back to what you've learned. Mentoring adds value to your life and the lives of those you touch. In order to teach something, you must understand it. The more you teach the more dialogue you establish. This dialogue encourages collaboration which invigorates ideas. They become better, more encompassing, more finely detailed. Both parties learn from the mentoring exchange. As it unfolds, your own expertise is honed by articulating the processes you developed and the forward thinking you now incorporate into your ideas. Who will you teach? Will you mentor family and friends on a personal basis, or will you share your knowledge to large groups through presentations, blogs or by writing a book about your expertise?

You never know what you might become good at, unless you overcome your doubts and take a shot. Try a few things. You may become good at something just because you like it, take an interest in it and then develop a level of expertise. Put in the time. Sweat a little. The worst that can happen is you will learn something. You've already proven that you have it in you.

Best Practices

"What's the take-away? What did I learn from the experience?" Architects refer to this thought schema as the establishment of best practices.

What are best practices? According to the American Institute of Architects (AIA), they are, "The collective wisdom of AIA members and related professionals. As a group they are:

- A compendium of relevant knowledge gained from experience
- Immediately applicable to a task at hand
- Distilled to their essentials
- Usable information
- Linked to related resources
- Kept relevant and up-to-date by inviting feedback from practicing professionals

The scope of knowledge and information that can be included in the AIA Best Practices is unlimited. The collective knowledge of AIA and allied members is a realm that is constantly expanding."

In the field of architecture, these best practices can include such topics as managing the small firm, project management, professional development, legal directives, client relations, building codes, sustainability and scores of other programs.

In life design, your best practices are the lessons you have learned that you can apply in future endeavors and pass along to your progeny. If you don't have children you can share it with friends. Best practices are the trying of new ventures, the building of networks or the joining of social and professional organizations. They help you to envision your big shiny purpose.

It takes time to develop a purpose, especially for something as big as life. The sense of purpose for an architectural firm blooms over time as the principals of the firm identify the mission. They establish their practice and professional acumen They satisfy clients, compete in contests, publish their ideas, and build a body of work. Finally it all culminates into a vision, not a vision for the next project, but a super-vision that directs the path of their practice, an amalgam of ideas, sensibility, science and a desire to improve the world. Architecture becomes.

My Favorite Physicist

My passion is to enlighten people to the concept of living an extraordinary life.

The extraordinary life does not re-tilt the axis of the earth. Rather, it is one that is not satisfied with routine and seeks an existence that is just that little bit beyond ordinary. It is one benchmarked by minor elevations of personal habits that pull us above the commonplace. By living this way we can have an impact on the lives we touch. By doing so we can uplift entire societies. How? Be patient.

Before I discuss my favorite physicist, I will touch on positive psychology. Scientists have been studying the effects of an upbeat psyche on health and well-being, finally putting academia behind what Norman Vincent Peale knew 60 years ago. ("The Power of Positive Thinking" stayed on the *NY Times Bestseller List* for 186 weeks.) Along with the positive, scientists have also looked at the negative and have begun to calculate the catastrophic impact on our world healthcare systems caused by treating depression and other forms of mental illness. Dr. Kate Hefferon (no relation) is a Lecturer MSc of Applied Positive Psychology at the University of East London. In the book, "Positive Psychology" (Open University Press, McGraw-Hill Education) which she co-wrote with her colleague, Ilona Boniwell, Dr. Hefferon defines an extraordinary life in the terminology of her field, "... the new science of positive psychology, (which) aims to 'understand, test, discover and promote the factors that allow individuals and communities to thrive' (Sheldon et al., 2000). Positive psychology focuses on wellbeing, happiness, flow, personal strengths, wisdom, creativity, imagination and characteristics of positive groups and institutions." Her work looks at individuals and groups, how they thrive and how increasing the well-being of one has a positive effect on the other.

"...positive psychology is not simply the focus on positive thinking and positive emotions. It's much more than that. Indeed, the area of positive psychology is focused on what makes individuals and communities flourish, rather than languish. Flourishing is defined as 'a state of positive mental health; to thrive to prosper and to fare well in endeavors free of mental illness, filled with emotional vitality and function positively in private and social realms' (Michalec et al., 2009)." According to Dr. Hefferon less than 20% of adults meet the criteria of flourishing.

As to the idea of uplifting society, Dr. Hefferon discusses how, "inducing positive emotions, committing acts of kindness and enhancing social connections enable individual and societal flourishing, demonstrating the usefulness of the discipline for individual, group and community wellbeing."

Now on to the physicist.

Deborah Berebichez, Ph.D., is a theoretical physicist born in Mexico City who seeks, among many professional aspirations, to inspire young women to study the sciences. In her TEDx talk from November, 2010, Debbie Berebichez discussed the principle of <u>emergent behavior</u>. She defined it as occurring, "when a system composed of independent parts forms more complex behaviors as a collective." It is not just aggregate behavior, like sand becoming a beach, but that which is different from the sum of its parts.

I tried to adopt the concept of emergent behavior for personal development, assuming we could examine our core behavior pattern and view it as a cooperative of activities that can each be improved upon; then collectively, what would emerge from the incremental improvements would be a person that is exponentially different from the individual who began a quest for personal growth. I thought I stumbled upon a brilliant idea, that is until I met with Debbie, who kindly pointed out the fundamental flaw in my theory. She explained that the definition of emergent behavior means all the component parts must be the same, such as cars in traffic. Emergent behavior arises from the collective of like components. In my hopeful but misguided idea, the elements of collective habits are diverse, driven by differing needs, desires and emotions. So even though my heart was in the right place; my science sucked. Now what?

Fortunately she is a patient mentor.

Her solution? Optimization: In her work as a quantitative analyst in the financial industry, (yes- she is also a wiz with numbers) Debbie Berebichez works with clients to optimize their investments. Essentially, she examines a financial strategy and make changes where necessary to increase the vitality of the whole. The difference in her work as compared to other models is that she looks at the pieces of an investment plan individually, including risk tolerance, diversity, cost, transaction fees, time frames, market trends, etc. and then only proposes to change what is necessary or amenable to the client to create the best possible overall investment strategy.

In terms of personal development, she says people must look at all aspects of their lives: intellectual pursuits, finances, personal and family relationships, personal fulfillment, community participation, wellness, and other elements along a broad spectrum, and then concentrate on fixing those areas that require the most attention. She basically scolded me for assuming that everyone has lousy reading habits, or needs to get healthier or has crumby family relations. These things are obviously not true for everyone. Individual needs, desires and perceptions vary and so should the individual strategies for optimization.

But I do believe that tweaking those areas of your life that need the most attention will bring other behaviors along, making your total package better. Have you ever bought a new exercise machine after seeing an infomercial? They always give you their "jumpstart" diet plan as a free bonus for "acting now." That diet has as much to do with your weight loss as the silly contraption. It's the general enthusiasm of a new program that has you eating fewer cookies, taking the stairs and drinking more water, which can lead to some initial loss of fat. One improved routine inspires the participation of others. I lost eight pounds when I stopped having beer and donuts for breakfast.

Honest self reflection is the key factor in arriving at optimized behavior. You must begin the process with a realistic assessment of the individual behavior patterns that make up your collective self. This is not easy to do given our reluctance to be honest with ourselves and our knack for self-delusion. (Most guys think they're about 40 sit-ups away from six-pak abs.) But try we must; for only through pig-headed determination will we break the tyranny of mediocrity. It is the hardest part of the process but one that will inevitably inspire emulation among friends and family and extend to neighborhoods and beyond. Cultural development begins with individuals making small changes across the spectrum of daily behaviors. Those changes spread within our circle of influence and that influence can have an impact on communities.

Self-Check

We can't change until we know what we want to change, such as what we take an interest in, which television shows we watch, the amount of time we spend watching television, the books we read with our children, our effort to exercise, our relationships, the discussions we have with our friends, the challenges we present to ourselves and the amount of over-indulgence or celebrity gossip we contribute to. We have become a society driven by trends, led like lemmings over the cliffs of banal. (The Cliffs of Banal are on the Canadian side of Lake Huron.)

For example, without reality TV, most thinking humans wouldn't concern themselves with the inane lives of certain New Jersey housewives, but popularity fosters interest from the collective, not just to gawk at the object of the popularity but to be a part of the throng, to not miss out. This celebrity-driven behavior is detrimental to our society. Am I being melodramatic? No. Time is finite. It's simple debits and credits. For every minute we spend watching this dribble we steal from our future a minute we could be spending in search of the extraordinary. When one adult watches this kind of television, they promote that activity to their children, who then develop the same unproductive habits they pass on to their offspring. Soon, we devolve into a society that is falling behind the rest of the developed world in math, literature and the sciences.

OK I'm out of the pulpit. On the positive side, extraordinary people conduct themselves in a way that is inspiring, challenging, and rewarding. They create a higher standard for themselves than they expect from others. They are fun to be around. They attract like-minded people. I've had the good fortune of sharing meals with Debbie Berebichez and Karen Tse. They are interesting, funny and wicked-smart. They make you think. Spending time with them inspires you to improve, to be better at something today. That kind of influence should be pursued at whatever level is possible for you. I'm not saying to ditch your friends. I'm saying, once in a while you should try to spend a little time with people who challenge you, to absorb their viral energy and spread it around.

The important thing is to take an action, no matter how small. Don't just accept things as they are. Be the driving force behind your life. You can't blame your circumstances if you're the one who creates them.

What does this have to do with our central, architectural theme? What I'm striving for here is to demonstrate a behavior that I believe is important for exploring creativity, which is to apply a cross-discipline philosophy, such as asking how architects can inspire personal development, or as Dr. Berebichez and her colleagues wonder how science plays a role in our everyday lives. Steven Johnson taught us in his book, "The Ghost Map", how a cholera outbreak in 1854 London helped to create the sewer systems which eventually saved large cities. New perspectives reveal discovery.

So how does architecture play a role in optimization? Can the dynamic of these basic architectural elements: volume, light, and flow, create an environment for optimal behavior? Do we engage our work or studies better in a space conducive to peak performance? Can the physical space encourage creativity and productivity? I believe it can.

A guiding philosophies of KPF Architecture is to build environments that allow the inhabitants to "be the best they can be, at what they do, within the space created for their purpose." Doesn't a physics lab need space to blow things up? Don't theaters need smaller backstage spaces to rehearse intimate dialog? Don't restaurant kitchens need easy access to fresh produce? Don't ideas need an environment within which to flourish?

As I mentioned in Level One, in Steven Johnson's book, "Where Good Ideas Come From," in which he describes platforms of creative breakthroughs, the 'places' where ideas happen. He wanted to know what the environment was for good ideas, "what was the space for creativity." What he discovered kind of vindicates the premise of The Seventh Level in case some of you reading this are still doubtful. "Most hotbeds of innovation have similar physical spaces associated with them: Homebrew Computing Club in Silicon Valley; Freud's Wednesday salon at 19 Bergasse; the eighteenth-century English coffeehouse. All these spaces were, in their own smaller-scale fashion, emergent platforms."

These were the spaces where the ideas that emerged were often markedly different from the components of ideas carried in by the travelers, the students and the businessmen. "The spaces...turned out to have these unusual properties: they made people think differently, because they created an environment where different kinds of thoughts could productively collide and recombine."

I said in Level One that to accept the premise of this book is to think of yourself as a place, not just in terms of design and systems, but as a place in which your temperament is approachable and inviting. It should be conducive to conversation, like the kitchen at a house party, challenging, creative and fun. It should encourage the free exchange of ideas and acknowledge that bad ideas aren't bad per se, but may just have bad applications. Your platform needs an open-all-night mindset, always willing to listen to new concepts and explore their possibilities.

The Kitchen Syncretic

Syncretism is a merger of religious beliefs. For example, Taoism is a mix of Buddhist and Hindu philosophies. If architecture were a religion, it would be a syncretic of ideas and science. Each element is advanced by the expanse of the other. Each one complements, suspends and tests the other, so that together they form an organism of innovation.

In northern India, the masterminds of Mughal architecture created iconic palaces like the Taj Mahal with a fusion of influences from India, Turkey and Persia. They represent the power of ideas in synthesis. It's what happens when ideas align with action, when intention meets initiative and when aspiration sizzles in perspiration. Your best life design will emerge when you bond emotional desire and methodology into a consciousness paradigm, with your work plans and success habits driven by your vision and identity.

You will stand back in awe of the changes you have made in your life, and you may even wonder how you managed to pull it off. You might think, "I really did that? Wow, that's just the best feeling ever. I've got to tell someone. But who? And what do I tell them? I want to tell them everything. I want them to know how hard it was at times, who helped me, guided me, supported me; how I managed to overcome obstacles and how I got my idea in the first place. How did I finally confront my biggest fear? How did I expand my brain power?"

The answer lies in understanding synergy.

Synergy is a neat word but it's overused in the corporate world. It seems every other hi-tech or progressive energy company has some offshoot of the word in their name (syner-link, synerjuice, sun-ergism, optimus synergus). Synergy has a variety of applications. It means the combination of two elements creates a functional advantage such as people or drugs working together. In chemistry it means the reaction obtained by the mixing of multiple chemicals is not just more effective but forceful, often explosive. When you unleash your creative brain and combine it with a voracious work ethic on all levels, incredible things can happen.

Science tells us synergy means that two forces once combined had an effect that were not possible if they remained separate. Your ideation needs it for fluency. Your internal synergy does not exist with desire alone and it will not work with ideas alone. Ideas require action or they stay in your brain. Desire requires focus or the energy is wasted. Together, ideas and desire create intention which compels action.

The architectural process is one that harnesses ideas and then focuses creative energy to produce sustainable results. You can apply it to any human endeavor you choose. The principles never waver. Becoming attuned to this effect underpins your goal for developing the best version of you; it closes the loop.

Every time you review a finished project, you prime the next one. Best Practices then becomes a tenet of your personal syncretic. It becomes a super-structure of the idea room, from which maximum performance will rise. Your life-sculpting ideas and evolving master systems will have a sort of hyper-genetic expression of the six previous levels. They will flourish because they will be launched from stronger, wiser idea structures. Level Seven creates a force amplifier.

Level Seven is the pinnacle of your process. In the construction trade, there is a celebration for the placement the last beam, or the last block of masonry. It is usually referred to as a topping out ceremony. Sometimes the tradesman who worked on the building sign the last beam before it's hoisted into place. In older European building traditions a tree branch or small pine tree is set on top to symbolize growth. That tradition has carried over into the United States.

So have your own topping-out celebration. Get your shovel and plant a tree. Have a ceremony. Have a drink; have a few. Invite your friends over to share a meal. Relish it with all the mustard or as Randy Gage says, "Out loud and in color." Daniel Libeskind says architecture is impassive, "expressive spaces are not mute. Silence is good for cemeteries, not cities." The freedom to express ideas is a privilege that Americans sometimes take for granted. Immigrants like Daniel Libeskind know the power of this freedom and live it fully every day. They are exceptional because The United States is an exceptional place, a place for free ideas to flourish. Real freedom comes from within, but American freedom lets you shout it out.

You are almost through with your first step in working your life design. Now you must go back and build your levels. Pick something that churns your blood. "You have to have ultimate passion;" says, Brad Cloepfil, "you have to love making architecture. You have to love drawing. You have to love the labor of architecture...It takes an uncommon commitment."

You have to love the process as much as the goal. Honor the work. Then celebrate your mission, your future growth, and your extra-ordinary life.

Ultima Cogitatio

Brad Cloepfil has a way of expressing his thoughts about architecture that is directly reflective of the underlying sentiment of this book. He says, "The primary responsibility of architects and the primary possibility of architecture is to create awe; to establish a sense of wonder, to provide a kind of emotional range in the world that no other art can provide." This is my hope for you, for us; to design a gift for our own lives and the lives of our children, to create something that shines on the other side of possible.

We expect from architecture as we do from our fathers, two virtues: first, that they do what they should and second, that they do it with style.

My father died in 1968 when I was eight years old. At just forty-one he was the first of seven siblings to pass. I remember him telling me (after I screwed up) that I wasn't working to my full potential. Actually, it was more like, "Jesus, Mary and Joseph! Use the brains God gave you for Christ's sake." Ahhh, memories. My father was a rough-and-tumble kind of guy, not an eloquent speaker or an intellectual. He fought for the Navy in World War II, became a truck driver and eventually, a police officer in the city of Newark, where he married my mother. Together they had four children. He died of heart failure. His life wasn't extraordinary, but he loved his kids, and he wanted them to do what they were capable of. That's not a bad principle to echo. Try it for a while and you will be amazed by what you're capable of. Do the amazing, and you'll never look back.

We expect our dads to do the right thing, to yell at us when we mess up, to bring us to ball games, teach us to change a flat tire and be the toughest guy we'll ever meet. We need heroes, and dads fit the bill just fine.

But I also think we want our dads to have style. That doesn't mean that they wax their eyebrows, shave their arms or wear silk under-shorts, but they should know enough to wear a pressed shirt and jacket to a wake. They should have a good haircut but not dye it, and while we're at it, unless you're Willie Nelson please, no pony tail. They should take their shoes off in your house and leave their shirts on at home. Having style means they shouldn't take themselves so seriously and they should make us laugh. They should know when to wink, have a touch of swagger. They should dance terribly, but dance anyway. At family parties my father wore these red socks with embroidered foamy-head beer mugs. They were hideous, but I suppose they had a certain tavernesque style to them. Dads should be good citizens and do a few things with flair. They should know how to make pancakes and grilled cheese. They should talk to us. They should be curious about the world but know simple pleasures. Enjoy what they are and nothing more. Feel the romance of a moment. Dads should always fall on the right side of a moral argument, because character counts, because human kindness is essential.

General Norman Schwarzkopf said, "The truth is, you always know the right thing to do; the hard part is doing it." So do the right thing, but have fun, have a little style. Get a new suit, and not from Sears. Stay healthy and vigorous. Break your routine. Eat a dragon fruit. Visit another country. Celebrate the Holi. Take part in a burning bowl ceremony. Go to Chicago. Have a sense of tragedy. Read Joan Didion. Why Joan? This is what she wrote about getting yourself involved in the only life you'll ever have, "I'm not telling you to make the world better, because I don't think that progress is necessarily part of the package. I'm just telling you to live in it. Not just to endure it, not just to suffer it, not just to pass through it, but to live in it. To look at it. To try to get the picture. To live recklessly. To take chances. To make your own work and take pride in it. To seize the moment. And if you ask me why you should bother to do that, I could tell you that the grave's a fine and private place, but none I think do there embrace. Nor do they sing there, or write, or argue, or see the tidal bore on the Amazon, or touch their children. And that's what there is to do and get it while you can and good luck at it."

Cheese and rice - she's good.

Here's a Myth

Either you are contributing to the betterment of society or you are a seeping waste of flesh. OK, so maybe it's not an actual myth but it could be. Some of you think productivity comes only in extremes. You are either the star athlete or the big dent in the recliner, the rock star or the whiskey-livered air guitarist, the astronaut or the guy who throws paper planes at his coworkers. I once asked a civil service acquaintance why he hadn't set his retirement date, given that he had put in the required time for a full pension. His response spoke to the kind of mindset that drove me to write this book, "What am I going to do, sit on the couch all day?"

"Well, no. I mean... What? Are you serious?"

Why, oh why, is a mute, stagnant, boring and slow decline into senility the only option? So what he is saying is...unless he is required to perform some function; he has no ambition to do anything else. Unless he is getting paid to turn out some mandated work product, he produces only flatulence. He has no plans, no interests, no hobbies or desires whatsoever. He has no urge to get out of bed except to move to the oatmeal. It doesn't have to be that way folks. The state of the world demands your involvement.

Look, accepting the premise of this book does not obligate you to be Catherine of Aragon or Siddhartha. There is no rule that says unless you aspire to be Jimmy Wales or Simon Cowell, you are doomed to a life akin to dry, white dog shit. (Simon Cowell? Don't laugh. Cowell has earned over 300 million dollars being savvy, insightful, intuitive and downright uncanny in his ability to discern what both the British and American pop-salivating cultures will fawn over.)

However, what this book does obligate you to do is to make a real effort toward achieving that which will make you fulfilled, without so much as an intimation of an excuse for inability. It obligates you to try something, anything that might make you feel like a bigger piece of the bigger picture. Once you read this book and proclaim your idea, you forfeit your right to make excuses. This book vanquishes the following BS excuses: time, genetics, birthplace, skills, education, luck, fortune, ethnicity, talent, height, looks, skills, family and daddy's lack of money. They're all gone - sorry doofus. You can either make progress or make excuses, but you can't do both.

There is not one thing on this list that can't be overcome with ideation, planning and effort. Stop belly-aching about why you can't do something and direct that energy to what you can do. Simon Cowell is wildly successful because he 'gets' popular culture. He has figured out what drives us. But the unique and vital skill he possesses is insight ability. He has proven many times over that he can study our western culture and determine the kind of entertainment that's missing, then he works to fill that need. He has it all figured out, without discounting the fact that fame and wealth are fleeting and that if you want sustained success you have to put in the hours. You have to be self-reliant, relentless and astonishing, even to you. He has a better work ethic than 98% of his fellow poser celebrities and the proof is in his 340 million dollars of earnings for his skills (by most estimations). He is one of the smartest people alive today, not because he cured cancer or invented a better micro-processor, but because he can do something that is typically accomplished only in retrospect, which is to identify the soul of his contemporary culture. But to say that Simon Cowell is merely gifted is an insult to his work ethic and principles.

So why the passing obsession with Simon? Because one axiom that he is emphatic about is - real success doesn't come easily. You must put in the hours, the work, the process of working your vision and staying resilient, even when things seemed stacked against you. The commitment for this new place you have built is not temporary, and the process will continue to get better. Dan Ariely could have stopped when he was burned and given up altogether. We would not have faulted him for that. He could have quit after acquiring his degrees; we would have applauded that. He could have stopped at teaching or writing or even publishing books. These accomplishments are admirable. But what is remarkable about him is he doesn't stop learning and will never stop giving through his lectures and writing.

My commitment to the power of me doesn't end at my desk. It extends to my children, Kaitlin and Jackson, and to my grandson Lucius. When you build something to last, the consciousness of that creation carries through generations. It sets examples. It has value.

If you've gotten this far you have proven to yourself that something significant is within your reach, and even if you didn't do it perfectly well the first time around, you have worked on the habits of mastery that will make the next project even better. You will be better for it...and that my friends is extraordinary. What you have built will last into the next generation and be the inspiration for the ideas of those who follow you. It's one, good, sustaining idea, followed by the conviction that acting on ideas is not wasted effort.

Whether to Wabi or Sabi

Wabi sabi is a Japanese aesthetic philosophy. It revolves around three central thoughts - everything is: imperfect, impermanent and incomplete. On Level Seven you can adopt this philosophy to accept that you can move forward without the plan being perfect. You can appreciate the exploration and the process of working the plan, even if you don't precisely hit your mark. There is nobility in trying, a sense of triumph in all endeavors that are heartily pursued.

Wabi sabi celebrates simplicity, the profound elements of nature and natural causes. It is imperfect and asymmetrical, like a tree, yet elegant, long-lasting and beautiful. It holds memories in its boughs, of the little Joey that climbed into his favorite spot, away from the noise of the city, to read the adventures of "The Fantastic Four." It's the difference between a 300-year-old Japanese garden and a pre-fab Tiki bar. It's the difference between the heavy old wooden bench in your grandma's kitchen and stackable plastic chairs. It's Grace Kelly vs. Kelly Kelly. Beauty is radiant and tactile, not airbrushed. But this is a western rendition of the term.

Some Japanese differ with the rather symbiotic western definition of wabi sabi, arguing that the terms are mushed together because they sound good as a pair, like zig-zag or Steve and Edie. Wabi and sabi are distinct terms. Wabi sabi is a composite of two concepts: wabi - which is a quietness attuned with nature in a simple despondence, an ascetic, monastic lifestyle; and sabi - which is the withered beauty that attends age, like a patina, chill and solitude. Both terms are better translated to describe feelings, rather than objects. To some westerners, wabi and sabi together evoke a reverent austerity, wisdom, an appreciation for what is known to be good, rather than a longing for what may be missing. A respect for authenticity and a shedding of accoutrements (pronounced with the requisite yet pretentious French accent).

To a Japanese, wabi sabi is described as more of an inexplicable feeling than a physical trait. According to Tim Wong, Ph.D. and Akiko Hirano, Ph.D., "Westerners tend to associate wabi sabi with physical characteristics - imperfection, crudeness, an aged and weathered look, etc. Although wabi sabi may encompass these qualities, these characteristics are neither sufficient nor adequate to convey the essence of the concept. Wabi sabi is not rigidly attached to a list of physical traits. Rather, it is a profound aesthetic consciousness that transcends appearance. It can be felt but rarely verbalized, much less defined. Defining wabi sabi in physical terms is like explaining the taste of a piece of chocolate by its shape and color to someone who has never tasted it." Martin Mull is credited with saying, "Writing about music is like dancing about architecture." I think that quotation expresses the inexpressibleness of wabi sabi.

Wabi sabi is an understanding that life is not endless, that all of us and all that is around us will return to the dust from whence we came. In that regard, wrinkles, cracks, stains and other signs of weathering are symbolic of the vital, the life once lived, the life enjoyed. It doesn't mean that you don't build with quality and don't care for what you have; indeed that is what makes our home and furnishings last and become part of our memories. It means if my son spills grape juice on my hand-made, Roy McMakin coffee table, I clean up the spill and then relish the staining as a memory of a relaxed afternoon having lunch with my boy. It's a memory that may have blended into the others were it not for that purple stain. It's caring for the good, solid stuff, without the need for ornamentation. It strips away gaudiness and leaves only what is essential. It is an ability to make do with less, without sacrificing love, kindness, laughter, caring and purposeful work. Above all, wabi sabi is genuineness. It's an Andrew Wyeth farmhouse.

I believe we have a natural yen for wabi sabi. You should pardon the pun. It's the only explanation for our near obsession with finding innovative ways to age things, such as chemically enhanced patinas, crackled paint, distressed furniture, barn-wood flooring, stone-washed jeans and other fake finishes. We want to feel the comfort of things that don't just look weathered, but are weathered, that have been cared for and lasted, that hold hugs and laughter in their energy and link us to simpler joys of youth. We want fulfillment, the satisfaction of a life well-lived. If we don't have these feelings we try to create them superficially. But here's the difference; being on Level Seven means that now you can create real things, that really last, that really count, that really matter to our authentic, genuine lives. The lives we share with the ones we love.

Do you have an Aunt Kate? I had one. She was actually my mother's aunt, the sister of my maternal grandmother. She was not an architect. She was not a writer or painter and never invented anything except perhaps a cosmic ability to project goodness. She was a beautiful person, sainted really. When I was 7 or 8 years old I would pretend to be a priest and say mass in her basement. She patiently guided me through prayers and took my salty communion crackers with reverence. Writing about those moments has ignited the remarkable human ability to remember details of distant memories if the attached emotions are strong enough, as these certainly are. Our seminal moments are all linked with emotion.

I have no memory of her as a young woman; she was always old to me. She "got the cancer" many decades after raising my mother, together with the orphaned nieces and nephews of her siblings, along with her own children, who were themselves abandoned by their father in childhood. My mother too was an orphan by 15 and part of this covey. They survived the depression, three wars, riots, layoffs, sickness, tragedy and hunger. They all grew to be productive members of our society, raising their own children and teaching them in turn, by living example, what the words fortitude and character really mean. She was a graceful and kind lady, resilient under invisible wings. She taught us all more than we can comprehend and won't until we face our own mortality. I loved her. The streets of heaven were quiet on the day she died.

I have nothing but fondness for any memory that rises from her spirit, but I also learned a lingering lesson in her final months. To watch a sweet person die a slow, painful death implants a sense of misery in your psyche that's hard to shake. It creeps around under the hedges and pokes you in the ankle once in a while, just to remind you that life isn't all margaritas and John Tesh. So we press on. We try harder. We strive to live a little north of the ordinary meridian, in a place that's sometimes scary, but always hopeful. To paraphrase the Native American teachings; we do not inherit this world from our parents; we borrow it from our children. Shame on us if we don't leave it a better place.

If we look at our own failures or the follies we've witnessed, they are usually preceded by one of two things, action without thought or the absence of character. If you follow the seven levels method, you will eliminate the two dominant causes of failure. The first three levels establish a process of thought and planning prior to taking action. Level Four is the bedrock of your character. Level Five is the action movie, not shot until the first four levels have been scripted. Level Six is the design of your daily routines, supported by your foundation and functioning to sustain what you have built through these thoughtful measures. The seventh level is the culmination of a well-worked design, and a lesson about character-based planning that you can pass on to another in your growing circle of influence.

Before writing this book I thought I admired the architects simply because I understood that they used both hemispheres of their brains so well. But now that I have performed my due diligence; my research has helped me transform the admiration into a profound affection for architecture as an exalted art form. It cocoons us while we think. It invigorates us while we create. It supports us while we dare. It is the tabernacle of our memories. I am grateful to the architects for their contribution to society and our cultural dignity. I have become enraptured by how the architect's artistic, holistic and progressive articulation of design is so naturally transferred to the philosophy of our extraordinary lives. I am now in hopes that by writing this book I have at least stirred some curiosity in the profession by those who hadn't previously considered it or had thought of it as only for the elite or the intelligencia. It is not just for poets; it is for all of us.

"Architecture is a small piece of this human equation, but for those of us who practice it, we believe in its potential to make a difference, to enlighten and to enrich the human experience, to penetrate the barriers of misunderstanding and provide a beautiful context for life's drama." - Frank Gehry

Do you want to make a difference? Do you want to live north of the ordinary meridian? Grab a pencil and start planning. I'll see you on **The Seventh Level.**

Appendix of Architects

A slightly irreverent appendix of my resources and the architects who are quoted or referenced, sourced primarily from Wikipedia and the web sites of their firms.

Saeema Alavi has been an architect since 1995. She has contributed to numerous projects in downtown Chicago, including Children's memorial Hospital, the Chicago Board of Trade and the East River Plaza. Saaema is a working mother of two, paints, plays the piano, speaks three languages... oh, and finds time to volunteer for the Central Asia Institute, which "empowers communities of Central Asia through literacy and education, especially for girls, and promotes peace thru education." If there is one thing that has struck me in researching this book, it's the unshakable work ethic and compassion of countless women who live and work well above the ordinary meridian.

Tadao Ando - Born September, 1941 - I like Ando because he is self-taught. He worked as a truck driver and a boxer prior to his design career. He won the Pritzker in 1995 and donated the $100,000 prize to the orphans of the Kobe earthquake. He has mastered the use of concrete which is prevalent in his designs. Most importantly, you just gotta love an architect who designed an art gallery for a beer company - Asahi Beer Oyamazaki Villa Museum of Art, Kyoto, Japan. He is a tough, wickedly smart craftsman who likes kids and beer. My hero.

Alejandro Bahamòn - An architect and writer of several books, he has teamed with artist Maria Camilla Sanjinés to publish their book, "Rematerial - From Waste to Architecture." He states, "Probably the most important challenge when recycling is to keep in mind that the reusing of materials should not waste more energy (water for washing, transportation, heating, etc.) than using a new material. Another challenge would be to know as much as possible about the properties of the materials in order to improve their functionality in their new use; this is a concept that some architects and designers are calling "super-use." In the book they discuss unique materials such as tire treads as roofing material and peach pits as flooring.

Daniel Burnham - (1846-1912) - was an American architect and urban planner. He was the Director of Works for the World's Columbian Exposition in Chicago. He took a leading role in the creation of master plans for the development of a number of cities, including Chicago and downtown Washington DC. He also designed several famous buildings, including the Flatiron Building in New York City and Union Station in Washington D.C. Frank Lloyd Wright said Burnham, "Made masterful use of the methods and men of his time."

Santiago Calatrava - Born in July, 1951, this Spanish architect is also an engineer, painter and sculptor. See what I mean about these guys? He designed the Allen Lambert Galleria in Toronto (that's in Canada). He designed the tallest building in Scandinavia, The Turning Torso building. He believes architecture should, "...not become a predator on the landscape, but rather gives dignity and human scale to its environment. Even in the most modest circumstances, there is the possibility for emotion and poetry."

David Chipperfield - Born December 18, 1953, Mr Chipperfield is a Londoner with offices in Milan and Berlin as well as his home town. He has been decorated with more than 50 prestigious architectural awards. Although I don't necessarily love modernist architecture; I love his philosophy - "We believe that high quality design results from the continuity of the design process and intensive dialogue. Dialogue with the client, consultants, contractors and other users. We work closely together to ensure that the best results are achieved through a synthesis of concept, beauty and functional integration."

Brad Cloepfil - An American architect born in 1956; Brad is the founder and principal of Allied Works Architecture in Portland, Oregon. Much of his work is centered around the arts and other cultural centers. His firm primarily designs museums, cultural institutions for education, and some creative business headquarters. His residential designs tend to be for people with extensive art collections. He is adamant about the type of architectural education that emphasises collaboration and cooperative learning from various artistic fields. Brad is a good role model for architects and other visionaries because although he clearly loves the process of working architecture, he remains open to multiple channels of influence, such as landscapes and sculpture that inform his work.

Paul Comstock - The only landscape architect in the appendix, Paul is as unique as some of his plants. From LandscapeOnline.com - "Paul Comstock, Managing Principal at Comstock LA, is a man of vision, creativity and spirituality of global proportions. He has designed gardens, habitats, amusement parks, museums and sports arenas all over the world. He has traveled five million air miles looking for just the right plant to be looked at, eaten, shaded by, listened to, or simply be energized and refreshed by. He has overseen the planting of more then 20 million trees and shrubs during his career. And they are all part of the many "sonatas" and "choral masses" he has composed. A horticultural genius, he worked for 16 years at Disney Imagineering as Director of Landscape Design, creating the landscapes surrounding many of the Disney theme parks, resort hotels and retail dining and entertainment venues worldwide, including the Disney's Animal Kingdom." In college he majored in mathematics, physics and fine arts. He is also a classically-trained professional musician and way-cool surfer dude.

Le Corbusier - (1887-1965) - He is considered a pioneer in modernist architecture and for that reason, he is associated with the kind of stark building design that creates a disconnect between the middle class and their appreciation of architecture. He too was an accomplished painter and designer of furniture. However, his abstract housing designs were too industrial for some tastes and his skill as an architect has made for heated debates among scholars.

Leonardo da Vinci - (1452-1519) He is perhaps one of the most diverse geniuses ever to strap on a pair of lederhosen. He was a sculptor, writer, painter, architect, musician, scientist, engineer, inventor, anatomist, geologist, cartographer and all-around swell guy. He was a vegetarian and is purported to have purchased caged birds only to release them. He created designs for machines of flight, water and land travel. He made discoveries in anatomy, civil engineering and hydrodynamics. He accomplished all of this in just 67 years, which is remarkable given how prolific he was. He was so advanced that many of his designs were not even feasible in his lifetime. If you learn nothing else from level one, learn this from DaVinci, "Iron rusts from disuse, water loses its purity from stagnation - even so does inaction sap the vigor of the mind"

Alex DeRijke - Dean of Architecture at the Royal College of Art in London. He balks at the notion that timber is a second-class cousin to concrete. Accepting that the 20th century was the era of concrete, he makes an interesting prediction, seen on his web-site - drmm.co.uk - "Timber is the New Concrete - This leaves the 21st Century open for the successor to concrete. My prediction is timber. Not any timber; not European oak, South American iroko or North American tulipwood, but fast growing softwoods, planted for laminating into large structural profiles. Currently these woods are the managed pine forests of northern Europe and Scandinavia. But, as global carbon becomes more about legality and commodity, and timber the site of hope and cash, Russia and China will start planting mega-forests on a scale the world has never seen."

Ellen Yi-Luen Do - (From her web-site) "Ellen is an associate professor in the College of Architecture, and the College of Computing, at Georgia Institute of Technology. Ellen received a Bachelors degree of architecture (Honors) from National Cheng-Kung University - NCKU in Taiwan, with a minor in Urban Planning, a Master of Design Studies from the Harvard Graduate School of Design - GSD, and a Ph.D. in design computing from Georgia Tech, with a minor in cognitive science & computer science. Ellen's papers have appeared in peer-reviewed international journals and conferences on computer-aided design in architecture, design studies, creativity, human-computer interaction, artificial intelligence, design computing and cognition, knowledge-based systems, computer & graphics, automation in construction and civil engineering. She has taught design methods and theory, readings in computational design and human computer interaction, design of computational design systems, computer animation, multi-media authoring, digital design media, graphics programming, modeling and rendering with computers, and introduction to computing in architecture..." Wow, I am truly impressed at the sheer voraciousness with which she produces. From a keynote speech she gave in Taiwan regarding the use of technology to guide us toward happiness, she said, "Achieving wellness is a Grand Challenge. We are concerned about the quality of life for ourselves and for our society. As human beings we want to develop and cultivate our untapped potential for a happy, healthy, creative and fulfilling life. Technological innovation may be just the key to unlock human potential for the Holy Grail of wellness."

Arthur Erickson - (1924-2009) Arthur Charles Erickson was a Canadian, which is kind of like an American, if everyone was from Minnesota. He was a modernist architect who studied Asian languages, which is unusual for both Canadians and Americans. Americans tend to think of learning foreign languages, especially hard ones like 'Asian' to be well... not worth the effort. We have the best movies, we invented rock & roll and we have the Dallas Cowboy Cheerleaders, so why doesn't everyone else - just speak English?

Matthew Frederick - He is the author of "101 Things I Learned in Architecture School." It has been one of the biggest sources of influence for me in writing about architecture because of its simplicity. Each of the 101 concepts is described on one page, yet he is able to capture the essence of each concept in just a few sentences. Agents and editors should have all their prospective client authors read this book to finally get that you can say a lot with few words. The brevity of each chapter opened my eyes to an array of architectural concepts, but also pushed me to conduct my own research to get a better understanding of the content to the point that I could describe it in my own style. I don't know if he did this on purpose, but it worked. For me it was a gateway work for exploring this profession of architecture, the process of creating it and the gift of artistry it provides.

Philip Frelon – (Born 1952) He was raised in Philadelphia and currently has offices in North Carolina. One of his notable designs is the Smithsonian National Museum of African-American Culture. He likes to expose the everyday person to the beauty of architecture. And he's married to a jazz vocalist, which makes him extra cool even for an architect.

R. Buckminster Fuller - (1895-1983) A classic American brain. He was a systems theorist, studying in a variety of disciplines and applying them across different professions. In that regard he probably would have liked this book. He was the second president of the Mensa Society back when it meant something to have a high IQ. In WWI he was a radio operator for the Navy and also a crash-boat commander (they rescue pilots who crash at sea). He also worked in the meat-packing industry and as a mechanic in a textile mill. Certainly he is most recognized for his brilliant geodesic dome, but I think his prescience is more telling of his intellect. Nearly 50 years ago, he predicted that society would be reliant on sources of renewable energy, long before it was hip to think so.

Jeanne Gang - (pronounced jeanie) A Chicago architect born in 1964. From her company web site; "Jeanne Gang leads Studio Gang Architects, a practice generating some of today's most innovative and creative works of architecture. Her projects confront pressing contemporary issues, including climate, urbanization, and technology. Published and exhibited widely, her work has been shown at the International Venice Biennale, the Smithsonian Institution's National Building Museum, and the Art Institute of Chicago. She is an Adjunct Associate Professor at the Illinois Institute of Technology where her studios have focused on megacities and material technologies."

She is widely credited with being an innovator in terms of making the best use of available products, even constructing buildings made from salvaged materials. Her Aqua Tower in Chicago is the largest project ever awarded to an American firm headed by a woman. This mixed use residential 82-story skyscraper practically drips with undulation. Is she extraordinary? Without question. And my mother's name is Jean.

Frank Gehry - Born February, 1929 - The Pritzker-Prize winning Canadian-American is considered to have produced some of the most important works of architecture in the 20th century. His architecture has been regarded as dramatic, spectacular, strange, out of context with the city, wasteful of structural resources and overwhelming of their purpose. But the one thing that struck me about Gehry was his reputation for his projects coming in on time and on budget, a rarity in his field. He attributes this to what he calls, "organization of the artist," which refers not to his planning skills, but to his presiding over the entire project from design through completion, nearly eliminating the types of bureaucratic interference that can slow down production and increase costs. Gehry said, "Take what comes your way. Do the best with it. Be responsible as you can and something good will happen, and it has."

Jonathan Glancey - is an architectural critic and design editor at The Guardian in the UK. Hey, less is more.

Paul Goldberger - Born December, 1950 - He is an architecture critic for the NY Times and he wrote one of the most influential works for my writing, "Why Architecture Matters." He grew up in Nutley, NJ, where many of my cohorts in law enforcement own homes. From Wikipedia - 11/11/2011 - "He lectures widely around the country on the subject of architecture, design, historic preservation and cities, and he has taught at both the Yale School of Architecture and the Graduate School of Journalism at the University of California, Berkeley in addition to The New School. His writing has received numerous awards in addition to the Pulitzer, including the President's Medal of the Municipal Art Society of New York, the medal of the American Institute of Architects and the Medal of Honor of the New York Landmarks Preservation Foundation, awarded in recognition of what the Foundation called "the nation's most balanced, penetrating and poetic analyses of architecture and design." In May 1996, New York City Mayor Rudolph Giuliani presented him with the New York City Landmarks Preservation Commission's Preservation Achievement Award in recognition of the impact of his writing on historic preservation in New York." He must look like DeGaulle when he wears all his medals. Goldberger has the stones and the credibility to take on titans like Donald Trump. About the idea of Trump building at Ground Zero, Goldberger wrote, "I think the challenge of Ground Zero goes beyond anyone's individual ego, and the problem of Donald Trump is he's never gone beyond his own individual ego."

Walter Gropius - (1883-1969) - Along with Mies van der Rohe and Le Corbusier, is a noted designer of modernist architecture. He designed the Pan Am building and is cited mostly for his work in establishing the Bauhaus School in Germany, which sought to bring together artists from many arenas and develop a total design philosophy that incorporated all forms of art.

Annie Han - The 44 year old Seattle-based architect formed the Lead Pencil Studio with her partner in order to evolve the interdisciplinary collaboration between art and architecture. She was born in Pusan, South Korea in 1967. Among her many endeavors, she studied sculpture for a year at Portland State University.

Steven Holl - Born December, 1947 - In July 2001, Time named Holl America's Best Architect, for "buildings that satisfy the spirit as well as the eye." On the 7thLevel he is known as a sage among sages, the capo di tutti capi of sages. He has won numerous national and international awards and contests. His philosophy has progressed from a more formal approach to architecture to the philosophy of phenomenology, which in this format I can only describe as the concept that building materials have sensory properties. The use of particular materials and their transitional relationships coalesce to form the character of the environment. Holl is also a water-colorist and is rarely without his sketch pad and the smart-phone he uses to send his ideas internationally to clients and colleagues. He is on the top of my gotta-meet list of architects.

Robert 'Bob' Hull - Not a Canadian despite the hockey name. Bob and his partner, David Miller, have earned over 100 awards and citation over 25 years. They are both fellows of the AIA. From the Miller-Hull web page, "As a founding partner of The Miller Hull Partnership with David Miller, Robert has been the creative force behind the majority of the firm's projects. An award-winning design architect, his experience on a wide range of project types goes beyond meeting the program requirements: it is a search for ideal solutions."

Louis Kahn - (1901-1974) - As an architect, Kahn was strongly influenced by ancient ruins, making his designs monumental, expressing the heaviness of the materials used in the construction. He is said to have worked closely with engineers which helped to make his work technically innovative and precise.

Eugene Kohn - Is co-founder of KPF (Kohn Pederson Fox) one of the world's largest architecture firms. I love this guy because he always considers the human element in his designs. "We create the environment that affects the lives of people." He was a naval officer which he credits with helping to develop the leadership skills necessary to run a firm of about 600 people. Whether he is speaking about running a great firm or designing a building, the sentiment is the same, "It's important to create an environment that brings out the best in people." He shuns fame. He never takes credit for an idea that someone in his firm came up with. He always thinks in terms of longevity, the occupants after the building is complete, the firm after he and his partners move on.

Tom Kundig - A Fellow at the American Institute of Architects, this 57 year old Seattle-based architect is one of the most honored men in his profession. From the profile page of his firm, Olson Kundig Architects, "Tom Kundig is one of the most recognized architects in North America. He has received some of our nation's highest design awards, including a National Design Award in Architecture Design from the Smithsonian Cooper-Hewitt National Design Museum; four National AIA Honor Awards; six National AIA Housing Awards; and an Academy Award in Architecture from the American Academy of Arts and Letters, which recognizes creative individuals whose work is characterized by a strong personal direction."

He is one of the few architects I would trust to design my home, knowing I would be thrilled with the finished product, without ever having seen the plans. That's a hint Tom, if you're reading this...Tom? Hello?

Daniel Libeskind - Born in Poland in 1946, he became an American citizen in 1964. Since I discovered him through TED talks; I will let them handle this bio. "A true renaissance man, Daniel Libeskind possesses a staggering array of creative interests -- he has been a free-verse poet, an opera set designer, a virtuoso musician. When he finally settled on architecture, it was not long (in architect-years, anyway) before he had taken the skylines of the world by storm. His many buildings include the recently opened Contemporary Jewish Museum in San Francisco, in the deep footsteps of his acclaimed design for the Jewish Museum Berlin -- his first major building project, and one of the most visited museums in Europe. He also created the spectacular extension to the Denver Art Museum (completed in 2006), and construction is under way on a massive retail complex on the strip in Las Vegas. Libeskind's ambitious and highly controversial design for the rebuilt World Trade Center is perhaps his most well known project, and despite almost a decade of political wrangling and bureaucratic whittling, he insists that the final design will retain the spirit of his original renderings."

Adolf Loos - Born in 1870, Austro-Hungarian architect Adolf Franz Karl Viktor Maria Loos, looked pretty much as you might expect from his name, but that doesn't mean he wasn't a fine architect. He was the favored designer of Vienna's elite. Diagnosed with cancer in 1918, his stomach, appendix and part of his intestine were removed. For the rest of his life he could only digest ham and cream. Inexplicably, I found that last bit hysterical, and I am somewhat ashamed of myself.

Ana Manzo - She is a beaming young architect from Venezuela, who writes poetically about her profession and seeks to understand the emotional underpinnings of the creative mechanism. In an essay, The Architecture of Emotion, she writes, "Much has been written about the way architecture affects people's emotions. But what if we look at it the other way? What about the way our emotions affect our designs?

On countless occasions we have heard (or said) the phrase "creative block." How many of those times has it actually been associated with an "emotional bloc?" It takes a lot of courage to open our hearts and express to the world how we feel at any given time, especially if the emotions that invade us, at that particular time, are negative. Some, those who dare, express themselves by crying, screaming, laughing, talking. But there are those too, who display emotion through creative expression (sometimes even unconsciously).

This theory has been discussed countless times from the point of view of art. And being how architecture is an artistic profession, creativity one of, if not the most important ingredient, it is logical to think that it too could be affected by our emotions. It is even possible, if we analyze architectural movements in history, that we would find clues suggesting that these movements were caused by the various situations (emotion-provoking) happening at the given time."

She uses the Level Seven philosophy of changing perspective to get a fresh take on a subject. She asks "what if?" which is all I ask of you; to ask yourself what would happen if you tried something different, something challenging or something scary. As Ana says, "Perhaps we do not want to admit that what we feel affects or influences our creations. We prefer to think that what we do is inspired solely by external agents . . . by emotions of others (the client), by the environment or by specific situations. Perhaps we dare not admit it, because we feel that this could weaken the seriousness of what we do.

But that is the easy way. I think we could see it as something positive and enriching, something that, if we learn to control it (reinforcing the positive emotions and limiting the negative ones), would be able to give a new level of emotionality to our buildings."

Roy McMakin - Roy is a Seattle-based artist, architect, designer and furniture maker. He was born in 1956 in Lander, Wyoming, which is just southwest of Where-the-Phukk-is-Civilization, Wyoming. Roy is a an artist with a sense of humor and a genuineness that sets him apart from some of his sublime colleagues. He is the first architect to respond to my request for an interview and he patiently worked with my awkward questions to help me elicit the best responses from him. His Wikipedia entry claims, "His art forces us to focus on the ontological complexities of furniture," which could be true if anyone actually knew what that meant. I think his residences and remodeling projects show his practical Wyoming side - there is a sense of warmth, quality and strength to his pieces - but they are elevated to artistry by his sense of color and innovation. Roy is a nice man. I am honored to claim his friendship.

Ludwig Mies van der Rohe - (1886-1969) His surname is actually Mies. He was a master of modernist architecture and well-known for saying, "Less is more." He is widely credited with creating the types of architectural forms that were in sync with a modern industrial society. Some of us look at modern architecture as representative of that kind of design style that average Joes feel distant from, but we must always look back on artists like Mies and remember to view their work from the perspective of their contemporary culture, recognizing that their culture may have been undergoing a sea change of zeitgeist and geopolitical paradigms. But I still can't get comfy on a concrete sofa.

Patrick Nuttgens - (1930-2004) - He was an English architect and academic who wrote many books on learning and design. He was stricken with poliomyelitis at age 12 but managed to recover after 2 years in the hospital. He went on to marry and father nine children, although he spent his last 19 years in a wheelchair. Presumably he fathered this lacrosse team before the whole wheelchair thing, but who knows for sure? His obituary in The Guardian included the following passage: "Patrick had a remarkable career by any standards, still more so for a man disabled, first by polio, and then by multiple sclerosis. From 1985, he used a wheelchair all the time. But always pithy and lacking in self-pity, he could communicate the experience of disablement with a rare ebullience and wit. "I may be a man of many parts," he said, "but some don't work as well as they once did." He claimed that he wanted to become an architect for his love of old buildings, not so much for his desire to design new ones.

Doug Patt - Doug is as much an entrepreneur as he is an architect. He pushes his creative juices through many channels He has produced a video series called <u>How to Architect</u> which opens up the day-to-day life of the architect to those who may be considering it as a career. He has written two books about architecture, the second of which is called "How to Architect" and will be published by MIT Press in 2012. He has worked on projects that have received American Institute of Architects (AIA) and Builders Awards in residential architecture."

He says of today's architecture, "Their structural gymnastics defy gravity, and their soaring spaces leave us breathless. Interior volumes transport us to another way of feeling and being."

William Pedersen - From the KPF site - "William Pedersen is the Senior Design Partner of KPF, which he founded in 1976 with A. Eugene Kohn and Sheldon Fox. KPF has earned the Architectural Firm Award from the American Institute of Architects and the Gold Medal of Honor by the New York Chapter of the AIA. Bill lectures internationally and serves on academic and professional juries and symposia. He is on the Board of the University of Minnesota Foundation and has been a visiting professor at the Rhode Island School of Design, Columbia University, and Harvard University. He has held the Eero Saarinen Chair at Yale University and has also been the Otis Lecturer in Japan. In 1989, he was honored as the Herbert S. Greenward Distinguished Professor in Architecture at the University of Illinois at Chicago. He has degrees in architecture from the University of Minnesota and the Massachusetts Institute of Technology."

Paul Raff - He began his Toronto-based practice in 1993. The firm is emerging as a leader is sustainable architecture and design. He became an architect because he "wanted to design unique and beautiful buildings." No surprise there. But he soon realized the enormous impact architecture can have on the environment, both in the immediate negative as well as in the drive to engender sustainability initiatives. Paul is the principal of the studio that bears his name. He was born in Montreal but grew up in the open-sky country of Canada's Saskatchewan prairies. Even though he later worked in the manic environments of New York, Hong Kong and Barcelona, and now lives in Toronto, he maintains his sensibilities about nature and landscape in his building designs. According to his company web site, "In 2001, Paul Raff became the youngest ever recipient of the Ontario Association of Architects' Allied Arts Award for lifetime achievement."

Hani Rashid - In 1989 he founded Asymptote Architecture with his partner, Lisa Anne Couture. The pair have lit up the design world with their innovative use of information-age technology. Hani Rashid received his masters in architecture from the Cranbrook Academy of Art in 1985. Within four years he was a teacher at the Columbia University Graduate School of Architecture, where he was also a leading researcher in architecture linked to digital technology. He has developed digital design programs and taught for many of the leading university architecture programs.

He was born in Egypt and raised in Canada, along with his brother Kareem, who is also an architect. He and his partner are world-class artists who design furniture as well as buildings. Their firm designed the wow-inspiring Yas Hotel in Abu Dhabi, the first hotel to span both a marina and a formula one race track.

John Ruskin – (1819-1900) Ruskin's influence as an art critic, writer and, philanthropist, thinker and environmentalist, is as strong today as it was in the last century. Many of the renowned architects credit Ruskin with informing their work.

I.M. Pei - Born 1917 in Guangzhou, China. He has been married for over seventy years – to the same woman. Nice. He is universally thought to be a master of modernist architecture. His career is bedecked with awards and accolades. He considers the JFK library, "the most important commission of his life." The same woman for 70 years?

Eero Saarinen (1910-1961) - Designed the main terminal of the Dulles International Airport and the Gateway Arch in St. Louis. He was born in Finland. Saarinen is equally noted for his furniture design, which further supports the idea of architecture as useful art. He died in his creative prime at 51 while undergoing surgery for a brain tumor.

Peter Sackett - Program Director of the AIA Seattle and contributing writer for The Seattle Times. He is a prolific writer about the architectural and design process. - "It's natural to view architecture as buildings, and never ask how they got there. Architecture is more than a tangible object - it is a long, complicated performance that transforms inspiration into physical substance."

Mark Sexton - From the Krueck-Sexton web site - "Mark Sexton is a principal and founding partner of Krueck and Sexton Architects. Together with Ronald Krueck, he designs and manages all of the firm's work. Mark is responsible for the development and execution of design ideas, and for the coordination of project teams. His dedication to craftsmanship, material, and detail enables the firm's built work to express the values of modern design with a timeless quality.

Mark is a Fellow of the American Institute of Architects and is a LEED accredited professional. He has lectured extensively and served on numerous architectural and design juries, both in the US and abroad. Mark is a board member of the Glessner House Museum, and is currently a student mentor at the Illinois Mathematics and Science Academy."

Louis Sullivan - (1856-1924) - He has been called the "father of the skyscraper" and a significant architect of the Chicago School, where he influenced people such as Frank Lloyd Wright. He lost his first job in Philadelphia because of the depression of 1873, so he moved to Chicago and played a pivotal role in the redevelopment of that city after the Great Fire. After many years of success, Sullivan, due to financial and personal catastrophes, died an alcoholic, broke and alone in a hotel room. A lesson here kids - for all he accomplished, he missed Level Six, the personal systems designed to sustain what he built.

He is credited with the phrase, "Form ever follows function," which to a non-architect like me seems almost painfully obvious. Did we really need him to declare this? Has anyone ever constructed a building and then figured out what to do with it afterward? Who paid for that project? Are there any buildings in major cities that serve absolutely no purpose, besides the UN?

Karen Tse - (pronounced - chĕh) is a remarkable woman. She is a person who fully uses all her talent and education to make a positive impact on the world. She earned her juris doctorate from UCLA and received a master's degree from the Harvard University, School of Divinity. Reverend Karen is a Unitarian Universalist minister and social entrepreneur, supported by several organizations, including Echoing Green and Ashoka. Out of an abiding concern for humanity, she travels throughout the world, visiting prisons, teaching defense attorneys and working with often hostile governments, in a valiant effort to stop the use of torture as an investigative tool. Through the law, she has been able to make lasting change. She says the rule of law is the bedrock to a stable society. In 2000 she founded the non-profit organization International Bridges to Justice. Their mission is noble, "We envision a world where the basic legal rights of every man, woman and child are respected in case of an arrest or judicial accusation, in particular: the right to competent legal representation, the right to be free from torture and cruel treatment, and the right to a fair trial. It's a world where the institutionalization of fair and effective justice practices have eliminated the use of torture as the cheapest method of investigation."

In 2008, the American Bar Association presented Karen with the International Human Rights Award. The chairperson stated, "She has been a leader in efforts to ensure that victims of torture and unjust legal proceedings can be heard and represented. Her work with the IBJ is proof that someone dedicated to a cause, with a clear vision, can achieve success against all odds." Please visit IBJ.org.

Robert Venturi - Born June, 1925 - Winner of the Pritzker Prize in 1991. His accomplishments radiate the international landscape. He is perhaps best known for having the onions to rebuke the stale, drab modernist architectural forms of the 50's and 60's. In response to the famous axiom of Mies van der Rohe, "Less is more," Venturi proffered, "Less is bore." Mies has since de-friended him on Facebook.

Harold E. Wagoner - (1905-1986) was an ecclesiastical architect who designed many churches in the United States, including the Cathedral of the Rockies in Boise, Idaho and St Marks Lutheran Church in Salem, Oregon.

Paul Williams - (1894-1980) Designed the Los Angeles International Airport and over 2,000 homes, many for Hollywood celebrities, in southern California. He was the first African-American to be a member of the AIA. Because he was black and his clients were mainly white, he believed they felt uncomfortable sitting next to him to show them his design ideas. He learned to write and draw upside down so he could sit across from the clients. "If I allow the fact that I am a Negro to checkmate my will to do, now, I will inevitably form the habit of being defeated." A true Level Seven mentality.

Frank Lloyd Wright - (1867-1959) - I was born in 1959, four months after Wright's death. A soulful coincidence? I think not. Just look at these parallels:
He was influenced by Japanese architecture - I like the work of Tadao Ando and I discuss the concept of Wabi Sabi in this book. Wright designed organic structures that were in harmony with nature - I take organic supplements. His work includes original and innovative examples of many different building types - my book is chock-full of examples of original and innovative architects. Wright authored 20 books - I authored 2, but have read many more. His colorful personal life often made headlines - mine has landed me in divorce court. And finally; Wright was recognized by the American Institute of Architects as "The greatest American architect of all time" - as for me... the AIA won't return my e-mails.

Gotta Love Wikipedia

Wikipedia is my Idea Platform - During the research of this book I regularly found myself on the pages of this spectacular tool founded by Jimmy Wales, one of the most astute of the contemporary big-brained Americans. The mission of Wikipedia, born in the imagination of its founder, is a world brimming over with free access to knowledge. James Donal Wales envisions it this way, "Imagine a world in which every single person on the planet is given free access to the sum of all human knowledge. That's what we're doing."

Whether I was watching TED Talks, reading about architecture and human development, or exploring the web, I would invariably look to Wikipedia or the sister sites such as Wikiquote and Wikiversity to learn what I could about a person, a place, a concept or historical reference, and then use that new information to find out more. I would use Wikipedia as a launch site to find other resources to confirm my ideas or source my quotations. The down side, if there is one, is that the platform is so vast you can get sidetracked. You find yourself skipping from one idea to the next and before you know it, you haven't worked on your own project in hours. But more often than not it helped me, inspired me, enlightened me and fed the muse. I watched a conversation among architects on ArchDaily. com in which Annie Han mentioned having a "wabi-sabi moment." Well I didn't know what that was but I was sure I needed to have one. Through Wikipedia I discovered an overview of the concept, links and references to other sources. Eventually I developed the idea that like wabi sabi, our missions and other life endeavors need not be perfect to be just perfect for what we require and life, like this book, is impermanent and incomplete. The concept is something we should embrace in striving to reach beyond the ordinary. We need to find joy in trying and satisfaction in the process. Along the way, some of us, the rare intrepid souls like Karen Tse, will live a life that truly compels unheralded acts of human kindness in the face of human misery; but all of us will find a rising satisfaction that is absorbed through the taproots of our consciousness.

From Wikipedia programmer Brandon Harris, "I don't think there will be anything else that I do in my life as important as what I do now for Wikipedia. We're not just building an encyclopedia. we're working to make people free. When we have access to free knowledge, we are better people. We understand the world is bigger than us, and we become infected with tolerance and understanding."

Wikipedia, like your brain, is a place of discovery, a place to begin the search for the greater good, a place that operates well north of that ordinary meridian. There is greatness in the possibilities of open-source knowledge and greatness within you. The possibilities for expanding Wikipedia are only outclassed by the possibilities of the human brain, as long as there is hope within the human heart.

My Roster of Inspirational Books

Why Architecture Matters - Paul Goldberger
The 7 Habits of Highly Effective People - Stephen Covey
Mozart's Brain and the Fighter Pilot - Richard Restak
The Secret Life of the Brain - Richard Restak
The Fountainhead - Ayn Rand
Dave Barry Turns 40 - Dave Barry
Awaken the Giant Within - Anthony Robbins
How We Decide - Jonah Lehrer
On Writing Well - William Zinsser
The Elements of Style - Strunk and White
Outliers - Malcolm Gladwell
The Tipping Point - Malcolm Gladwell
Blink - Malcolm Gladwell
All the Pretty Horses - Cormac McCarthy
The Crossing – Cormac McCarthy
The Road - Cormac McCarthy
Discover Your Genius - Michael J. Gelb
101 Things I Learned in Architecture School - Matthew Frederick
A World Lit Only by Fire - William Manchester
The Power of Intuition - Gary Klein
Sources of Power - Gary Klein
Why Smart People Can be so Stupid - Robert Sternberg
Sparks of Genius - Michelle Root-Bernstein
Where Good Ideas Come From - Steven Johnson
Emergence: The Connected Lives of Ants, Brains, Cities and Software - Steven Johnson
A Whole New Mind - Daniel H. Pink
Use Your Brain to Change Your Age - Daniel G. Amen

Poems
The Marshes of Glynn - Sydney Lanier
Annabelle Lee - Edgar Allen Poe
The Raven - Edgar Allen Poe
Mnemosyne - Trumbull Stickney
Do Not Go Gentle Into That Good Night - Dylan Thomas

Writers
Cormac McCarthy
Joan Didion
Pete Hamill

Websites
TED.com
archdaily.com
bigthink.com
psfk.com

About the Author

Joe Hefferon lives for the juxtaposition, to see ideas and emotions working well together when they shouldn't. It's a running theme in The Seventh Level, to join forces with unlikely allies, to always seek a fresh perspective. Joe dreams a lot and remembers many of them, often for years. Some are quite vivid, most are dark. He doesn't know if it's connected but he writes from an emotional, not an academic viewpoint.

Joe is a recovering civil servant, trying to learn how to be imaginative and to be disdainful of tedium. He has two children he adores. He wants to open their eyes to possibility. To art, language, science, nature and the human spirit - that's where he wants to lead them.

Joe lives and works in New Jersey. Don't hold it against him.

Joe's first book, a noir crime novel, "The Sixth Session", was the Police-Writers.com Book of the Year for 2010.